The Pilgrim's Journey

Overcoming Spiritual Emptiness and Discovering God's Plan

GERARDINE E. OBIEGBU-ACHORONYE

ISBN: 979-8-9987085-1-0 (Paperback)

ISBN: 979-8-9987085-0-3 (Hardcover)

ISBN: 979-8-9987085-2-7 (eBook)

Book design by Dara Publishing LLC

Place of Publication: Irvington, New Jersey, 07111

Library of Congress: 2025908377

Printed in the United States of America.

Disclaimer: The publisher and the author do not make any guarantee or other promise as to any results that may be obtained from using the content of this book. This publication is meant as a source of valuable information for the reader. However, it is not a substitute for direct expert assistance. If such a level of assistance is required, the services of a competent professional should be sought.

DEDICATION

This book is dedicated to the Blessed Mother Mary. She was my first evangelizer, the one who spoke to me in a gentle, still, but compelling voice, "I want you to follow my son," and I did. Honoring her invitation commenced my formal journey of faith with God which has made me who I am today and the experiences have given birth to this book,

The Pilgrim's Journey.

THIS BOOK ENDORSEMENT

Gerardine E. Obiegbu-Achoronye graduated with a Bachelor of Science Degree Second Class Upper Division (2.1) in Government and Public Administration from Imo State University. She also holds a master's degree in Public Administration from Lagos State University, where she graduated with a Second Class Upper Division and a cumulative aggregate of 4.2.

Gerardine is a compassionate and humble individual who understands the complexities of faith and the courage it takes to grow spiritually. She writes with openness, values authenticity, and embraces vulnerability to connect with her readers.

In her book *The Pilgrim's Journey*, Gerardine takes readers on an evocative journey through the highs and lows of a Christian's spiritual life, centering on a personal narrative that is as relatable as it is inspiring. This book is a reflection on faith, resilience, and growth in the face of life's challenges. It feels like a conversation with a friend who has opened her heart to share her story—an honest account of a Christian pilgrim's life that will likely resonate with anyone who has ever faced doubt or struggle, or who has been endowed with a renewed sense of divine purpose.

This book is deeply rooted in a personal tone. The author doesn't just tell readers what faith should look like; she shares her own story with humility and openness, detailing her transformation from a place of spiritual "ignorance" to a life filled with faith and purpose. The language is gentle yet encouraging, inviting readers of all stages in their spiritual journey to find solace and inspiration. Particularly powerful are the descriptions of her "moments of sheer divine intervention." These experiences are recounted in a way that feels genuine—neither exaggerated nor overly dramatic—making them accessible and authentic.

The book is also structured in a way that reflects the stages of a journey, which makes it easy to follow. Each chapter reveals a new challenge or insight, akin to stepping stones guiding readers from one phase of faith to another. This allows readers to pause, reflect, and apply her lessons to their own lives. Her narrative offers a sense of companionship and warmth, a refreshing contrast to more didactic religious texts. It's an invitation for readers to journey with her, with every victory and setback serving as a stepping stone toward the ultimate destination—communion with God.

The Pilgrim's Journey stands out for its intimate storytelling, especially among other Christian spiritual journeys or memoirs that sometimes take on a more instructional tone. Its style is reminiscent of classics like John Bunyan's *Pilgrim's Progress*, yet it's refreshingly contemporary and relatable. While Bunyan's allegorical journey explores the Christian life through symbols and metaphors, *The Pilgrim's Journey* is grounded in real, lived experience that readers can visualize and empathize with. Unlike other Christian self-help books that can feel prescriptive, this book focuses on bearing witness to God's work in a single life, reminding readers that each Christian journey is unique, with its own trials and revelations. It's less of a "how-to" guide and more of a companion text—a book that provides comfort and encouragement rather than strict doctrine.

Meanwhile, let me testify that while reading this book, there was a moment that spurred me to test the veracity of her statements. I had an assignment at my workplace that everyone depended on to move a project forward. Before reading this book, all concerted efforts to find a solution for this assignment were unsuccessful. This left the project unfinished. Then, I read this book and became so inspired that I asked God to show me a way out of the quagmire I was facing at work.

To my amazement, when I returned to the project, with just a little effort, the challenge unlocked and the problem was solved. Woah! Even my colleagues at work were astonished and asked how I was able to unravel the answer that saved the day. I was shocked too, but I knew within me that it was a miracle—an answer to the request I made to God based on the faith I built while reading *The Pilgrim's Journey*. Yes, God used this book to resolve an almost-stalled project, which made everyone happy and granted me the success I needed at the workplace.

The Pilgrim's Journey is a beautifully heartfelt book that will appeal to Christians seeking encouragement and affirmation in their walk of faith. Its strength lies in its simplicity and sincerity. It is not only an account of one woman's spiritual journey but also a gentle invitation to others to find meaning in their own path.

This book is best suited for readers who appreciate a narrative that feels genuine and unpretentious, providing inspiration without overwhelming them with doctrine.

For those looking to find a fellow traveler in their spiritual journey, this book will be a welcome guide and friend along the way.

Dr. Perpetua Emeagi (Ph.D.)
United Kingdom

TABLE OF CONTENTS

Foreword 11

Preface...13

Introduction 17

Chapter 1
Awakening From Ignorance 23

Chapter 2
The Unshakable Call Of God 29

Chapter 3
Signs And Wonders In The Heavens....................... 39

Chapter 4
Deliverance, Dreams, And Revealed Songs 45

Chapter 5
The Flow Of Amazing Grace 55

Chapter 6
Walking Through The Valley.................................. 63

Chapter 7
Testimonies, Teachings, And Words Of Wisdom 69

Chapter 8
Blessed Mother Mary: "White Lily"........................ 85

Chapter 9
Refined In The Wilderness 99

Chapter 10
The Faithfulness Of God, The Sower's Story, And The Rapture... 105

Chapter 11
And God Manifested His Presence.......................... 117

Chapter 12
Wisdom Passed Down From Dad.. 127

Chapter 13
Measuring Growth And Purpose.. 133

Chapter 14
The Power Of Prayer.. 139

Conclusion... 153

Author's Note 159

About The Author 161

Acknowledgement... 163

FOREWORD

There are people who live ordinary lives quietly, and then there are those who live with such brilliance, faith, and unwavering purpose that their presence becomes a testament to the divine. Gerardine E. Obiegbu-Achoronye is one of those rare souls. To know her was to witness a living flame burning with passion for God, radiant with intellect, and driven by a devotion that never waned. She is a woman of deep conviction, a scholar of uncommon brilliance, and above all, a pilgrim whose journey was marked by grace, revelation, and sacred pursuit.

The Pilgrim's Journey is more than a memoir. It is a spiritual landmark. In these pages, Gerardine invites us not just to observe her walk of faith but to walk alongside her. She opens the door to her inner life with honesty, reverence, and insight, reminding us that life is not a random series of experiences, but a divinely orchestrated pathway leading us closer to God's heart.

With elegant prose and profound humility, she recounts her transformation from knowing of God to knowing Him intimately. Her story resonates with every soul who has ever felt the tug of eternity, who has ever questioned their purpose, or who has dared to believe that a life surrendered can become a vessel of light. From mystical encounters to quiet revelations, Gerardine shows us that God still speaks, still guides, and still walks with His people.

As you turn these pages, you will feel her faith leap off the paper. You will hear the melodies God gave her spirit. You will witness a woman who did not merely survive life's valleys but emerged with songs, scriptures, and visions that became

11

spiritual bread for others. Her life was an altar, and her words now immortalized in this book are the incense that continues to rise.

Gerardine believes in the sacredness of the journey, not just the destination. She believes that we are not merely wanderers, not tourists, not spectators but pilgrims. Each of us, called and carried by grace, moving ever closer to divine communion. This book is her legacy, and now, her hand extends to you.

May you read slowly. May you listen deeply. May you walk courageously.

And may you, like Gerardine, find that every step—no matter how ordinary—can become holy ground.

By Ms. KeriLynn Lowenstein, M. Ed.

Ms. KeriLynn Lowenstein is an experienced United States of America school teacher, school sports coordinator, a successful and multi-faceted entrepreneur, and a doctoral candidate.

PREFACE

Life, at its core, is a journey—one that stretches far beyond the physical spaces we occupy or the milestones we chase. For the believer, this journey is not just about surviving; it is about awakening to the divine truth of who we are, why we are here, and where we are destined to go. *The Pilgrim's Journey* is my humble attempt to share that awakening—my walk from ignorance to illumination, from wandering to purpose, from striving in the flesh to thriving in the Spirit.

This book was not written merely to recount experiences, but to offer a light on the path for others who, like I once did, find themselves seeking something deeper. Perhaps you have heard an inner voice calling you to more. Perhaps you've felt the weight of emptiness even while surrounded by worldly success. Or perhaps you are already on your faith journey but in need of encouragement, clarity, or confirmation that you are not alone. Whatever has brought you to these pages, I want you to know this: you are not here by accident.

My journey began in what I now understand to be a life clouded by spiritual ignorance. I had knowledge, ambition, and confidence in my abilities, but I lacked true understanding of who God is and what He desired for my life. Like many, I mistook worldly comfort for fulfillment—until a moment of divine interruption changed everything. That call, stern yet loving, came not through a loud voice or grand miracle, but through a persistent inner prompting—a voice I came to recognize as the Blessed Virgin Mary, leading me toward her Son, Jesus Christ.

From that moment, everything began to shift. What started as a nudge became a transformational encounter with the living God. I began to see signs in the clouds, receive spiritual messages through dreams, and experience the presence of God in ways I had never imagined possible. These divine moments were not figments of imagination; they were tangible, powerful, and deeply personal experiences that shaped how I understand life, faith, and grace. In obedience, I began to document them—first for myself, then for others. This book is the result of that obedience.

As you read *The Pilgrim's Journey*, you will travel with me through chapters that explore seasons of doubt, divine dreams, miraculous deliverance, and the ever-flowing grace of God. You will witness testimonies of answered prayers, spiritual revelations, battles with unseen forces, and victories that could only be achieved by the hand of God. You will hear songs birthed in the spirit, encounter symbolic teachings rooted in scripture, and walk with me through wilderness experiences that tested my faith but ultimately deepened it.

More than anything, I want this book to be a source of light and hope. I want you to see yourself in these pages— not because our experiences are the same, but because our journey is shared. We are all pilgrims walking toward a greater purpose, and it is my prayer that this book helps you reflect on your own spiritual path, rekindle your relationship with God, or perhaps begin it anew.

This is not a perfect story, nor am I a perfect person. I am still on this journey. I still have questions. I still face trials. But what I have come to know—deep in my spirit—is that God's grace is sufficient. His love is real. And His presence is available to anyone who seeks Him sincerely. The same God who revealed Himself to me through scripture, signs, and songs desires to walk closely with you too.

Whether you are just beginning your journey, standing at a spiritual crossroads, or simply needing encouragement to press forward, I invite you to walk with me through these chapters. Read with an open heart. Reflect with a seeking spirit. Pray as you go. And above all, listen—to the still, small voice that may already be whispering to your soul.

This book is not the end of my story; it is just one marker along the way. And I believe, by God's grace, it will be a meaningful one for you too.

So, take my hand, fellow pilgrim. Let us walk together for a while, and let the Spirit lead us home.

With love and in faith,

Gerardine

INTRODUCTION

An Invitation to Walk with God

We are all pilgrims.

Not merely wanderers, not tourists, not spectators—but pilgrims on a sacred journey. Whether we realize it or not, life is more than a series of events or achievements. It is a divine pathway, marked by moments of struggle, revelation, and transformation, leading us ever closer to the heart of God.

The Pilgrim's Journey is not just the story of my life; it is the testimony of what happens when God calls, and we dare to answer. It is a reflection of how grace, faith, and obedience can turn ordinary steps into holy ground. It is a collection of deeply personal experiences, spiritual lessons, and divine encounters meant to awaken, guide, and inspire others along their own path.

My life didn't begin with spiritual awareness. Like many, I started in a place of ignorance—not due to a lack of education or intellect, but due to a disconnect from the true source of wisdom and purpose. I knew of God, but I didn't know Him. I had faith in religion but not yet in a relationship. I was pursuing life on my own terms, doing what seemed right, until an unrelenting inner voice began calling me—softly at first, then with increasing clarity and insistence. That call marked the beginning of my transformation, the start of my pilgrim journey.

Perhaps you've heard that voice too. Maybe you've felt an inner stirring, a spiritual hunger that no success, relationship, or achievement could satisfy. Maybe you've been walking through life feeling unfulfilled, or you've hit a point of crisis where everything you once trusted seems uncertain. If that's the case, I want you to know that you're not alone—and that there is a purpose to your restlessness.

This book is an invitation to pause, to reflect, and to journey with intention. It is not a theological textbook or a doctrinal manual. Rather, it is a spiritual memoir, a heartfelt offering of my walk with God, shared with the hope that it will illuminate your own walk.

Throughout these pages, you will encounter my raw, real-life experiences: moments of joy and deep sorrow, encounters with the supernatural, dreams and visions, personal struggles, and triumphant testimonies. You'll read about the time I first heard the voice of the Blessed Virgin Mary calling me to follow her Son. You'll see how signs in the sky, unusual dreams, and even birds at my window became messages from heaven. You'll walk with me through dark valleys of fear, pain, and spiritual attack and watch how God's grace carried me through every storm.

You will also hear the songs that God gave me in my spirit—melodies of hope that lifted me when words could not. You'll discover how I experienced the Holy Spirit not as a distant doctrine, but as a daily companion, teacher, and comforter. And perhaps most importantly, you'll witness how God's amazing grace transformed me, reshaping my priorities, renewing my mind, and filling the emptiness I didn't even know I had.

Each chapter in this book represents a stage on the journey. Some are mountaintops, others are valleys. Some are filled with light, others are shaded by confusion or sorrow. But through it all, one truth remains constant: God is present. He is guiding. He is speaking. He is waiting for each of us to respond.

You'll notice that many of the chapters include scripture and symbolic reflection. That is intentional. My journey was never disconnected from the Word of God—it was, in fact, rooted in it. Scripture became the lens through which I interpreted the signs around me, the tool for discernment when dreams came, and the source of strength when my spirit was weak. I believe the Word is alive, and when it comes alive in your heart, it will anchor you through every season of life.

You will also see references to the Blessed Mother, Mary. As a Catholic, I have a deep reverence for her role—not only in the life of Christ but in the lives of those she gently leads to Him. Her voice was instrumental in my awakening, and her intercession has remained a source of strength. I share this openly, knowing that God uses whom He chooses to reach our hearts.

Yet, despite all the visions, signs, and revelations I've experienced, I want to emphasize this: the journey is not about the miracles. It's about the relationship. The beauty of walking with God is not found only in the extraordinary; it is often discovered in the quiet moments of prayer, in the subtle whispers of the Spirit, and in the decision to trust when nothing makes sense. That is where faith grows. That is where transformation begins.

The purpose of *The Pilgrim's Journey* is not to impress, but to impact. It's not to elevate my experiences, but to encourage your faith. If God could reach me in my confusion, if He could deliver me from fear, heal me from pain, and speak to me in my ordinary life, He can do the same for you.

You don't need to have all the answers to begin. You don't even need to feel ready. You simply need to respond.

This book is a spiritual companion. As you read, I invite you to reflect, to pray, and to ask God to speak to you personally. Allow the stories to stir your heart, the scriptures to deepen your understanding, and the Spirit to draw you closer to your divine purpose. If you keep an open heart, I believe God will meet you in these pages—not because of me, but because He never stops seeking those who seek Him.

So, wherever you are on your journey—starting out, somewhere in the middle, or feeling lost altogether—take a moment. Breathe. Invite God into your reading. Ask Him to walk with you through each chapter.

This is not just my story. It is an echo of every pilgrim soul that longs for more. And together, we will journey, step by step, with grace as our guide, toward the One who awaits us with open arms. With deep love and abiding faith.

Gerardine E. Obiegbu-Achoronye

As you read along, think about these words:

'Like a well so deep; Like a sea so wide;
Like a tree so tall; Like a grass so serene;
The euphoria of Christ is so overwhelmingly refreshing;
The nature of God, who can explain?!'

Chapter 1

AWAKENING FROM IGNORANCE

"The people who walked in darkness have seen a great light; upon those who lived in the land of gloom a light has shown." Isaiah 9:1 (NABRE)

---

*E*cclesiastes 1:2 says: "Vanity of vanities! All things are vanity." Here was a man who asked for wisdom in order to apply knowledge. He knew everything that could be known, including the experience of affluence. He did all that could possibly be done, including satisfying the desires of human nature, as cited in Galatians 5:17–26. But eventually, after deep reflection, he realized he had not found fulfillment despite all his efforts in life. What a shame! Hence, he declared in Ecclesiastes 1:18 (New American Bible Revised Edition): "For in much wisdom there is much sorrow; whoever increases knowledge increases grief."

This account in Ecclesiastes perfectly illustrates life in ignorance. It depicts a state of spiritual ignorance—a lack of personal relationship with Christ—even when one is filled with philosophical knowledge.

Let me also reference Aristotle, who echoed Socrates, one of the foremost fathers of philosophy, when he famously said, "The more you know, the more you don't know." Socrates expressed it this way: "The only true wisdom is in knowing you know nothing."

In every pilgrim's journey, there comes a moment of profound confusion—a season of ignorance. During this stage, it may feel as though you are lost in a maze, with every decision clouded by uncertainty.

This season of ignorance often leads people to try out many things, only to discover with time that it is all in vain. It is a stage of experimentation, where one walks blindly in search of fulfillment. This was my own experience. At that time, life appeared to be good and satisfying. I had no sense of accountability. I justified my actions and believed they were acceptable. I lived in what I now call "a blank world"—a life devoid of true purpose and understanding. Although it seemed to be the best part of my life, it eventually left me with painful memories and deep regret. One could even call those years wasted. And though I sometimes wish I could erase those experiences, they remain part of my story.

Yet here is the key: reflect on this period with sensitivity and patience. Cultivate a deep sense of awareness, and pay close attention to the subtle signs that tell you it's time to move on. Understanding when one chapter ends and another begins is vital for the success of your journey. Embrace the stage of ignorance as part of your growth. Each experience, no matter how unclear, plays a role in shaping your path.

I believe that you, the reader, either have come through this stage or will come through it—victoriously. The memories from that season will one day serve as reference points to help you navigate other parts of your journey, just as they have helped me in countless ways.

As a pilgrim, I reached a point when I felt completely empty and yearned for something more fulfilling. This emptiness was not about lacking material things, because in this world, problems can often be "fixed" by worldly means—even through questionable actions. The world, in its ignorance, applauds shortcuts and mocks moral values. Those who dwell in this stage pride themselves in being "fast" or "smart," though their ways are far from divine.

For me, that sense of emptiness led to a divine quest to answer an inner call that I could no longer ignore. I felt compelled to discover the deeper purpose behind my existence. I wanted to understand why I was here in the first place. In other words, I wanted to know what my pilgrim journey was all about.

Paul, in Philippians 3:10 (NABRE), came to this same realization. He wrote of his desire: "to know Him (Christ) and the power of His resurrection and (the) sharing of His sufferings by being conformed to His death."

Have you ever felt that still, small voice within, gently asking you to surrender your heart? Perhaps you have heard someone ask, "Have you given your life to Christ?" Or maybe you've simply felt that still, small voice within, gently inviting you to surrender your heart. Whatever form it takes, the call is always a signal—it is time to realign your life and move to the next stage of your journey.

I, the writer of this book, heard that call deeply and persistently. The voice came with stern urgency, but also with a passionate and compassionate tone. It said: "I WANT YOU TO FOLLOW MY SON." At that time, I wasn't ready to leave my old way of life, so I made excuses. I insisted that I needed to pass my high school examinations and gain admission to college first. I even dared to question the voice: "Why should I follow your Son?" Yet I recognized the voice. It was the voice of the Blessed Virgin Mary, the mother of Jesus Christ.

I thought I had succeeded in postponing the call. But then I passed my high school exams—exactly as I had requested. I knew God was involved. Not long after, the voice returned: "You wanted to pass your secondary school examination. Now you have your results as you requested. So follow my Son."

At that moment, I knew the only honorable and truthful response was to obey. God had kept His word, and it was only right that I fulfill mine. I yielded. And I can say without hesitation, it was the best decision I have ever made in my life as a pilgrim on Earth.

I remain eternally grateful to that firm yet gentle, maternal inner voice, the Blessed Virgin Mary who first called me to Christ.

To My Fellow Pilgrims

This journey—our life's pilgrimage—is not one whose beginning or end we can fully determine. But what we can choose is how we make use of the time and opportunities given to us. That calls for deep thought, reflection, and careful navigation.

Eventually, every soul begins to seek understanding. A restlessness is stirred within, and we realize we don't know as much as we thought we did. The teachings of Christ become lifelines—illuminated paths for those seeking to live with a clear conscience. They may seem difficult, but they are not impossible when we take the step of faith and invite the Holy Spirit to be our guide.

Sadly, the world is often too busy, too noisy, to stop and reflect. Perhaps that's why there is so much chaos. Yet, a little pondering . . . a slight shift in perspective . . . a single act of honor . . . these could make the world a better place. Was that not God's intention from the beginning? He looked upon all that He created and said, "It was good." What, then, has happened to the people and the places He declared good?

Today, the "haves" want to take everything. The "have-nots" feel cheated and respond with destruction. What is the solution? If God desires true worship, why is it so hard to give it? If peace is what we desire, why does it feel so far from our grasp? If a selfless leader needs loyal followers, why is it difficult to achieve?

The answers to the world's deepest problems may begin with something simple: a moment of reflection, a conscious decision, a return to conscience.

I once spoke about the importance of conscience at my workplace. A superior officer brushed it aside, saying I should forget about conscience. But how can I? Conscience, I believe, is the foundation of all good moral reasoning. When the conscience is dead or ignored, the ability to think and act rightly becomes distorted.

So I urge you, let your conscience guide your decisions. That is the very reason God placed it within each of us.

Pause and Reflect

There comes a time in life when we realize that what we once thought was right was, in fact, a path of ignorance. Without true knowledge of God, we often chase after things that do not fulfill us, only to find ourselves empty and searching for something more. But when God's light shines on us, we awaken to truth, purpose, and a deeper understanding of His calling. Before moving on, take a moment to reflect on the themes which speak to a season many of us have walked through—when we chased fulfillment in the wrong places or lived disconnected from God's truth. These questions are meant to help you examine your own spiritual journey with honesty and openness. Write your answers in a journal or pray through them, allowing the Holy Spirit to reveal deeper truths about your path and purpose.

Reflection Questions

1. In what ways have you sought fulfillment through things that ultimately left you feeling empty or unfulfilled?

2. Can you identify a time in your life when you were spiritually unaware or disconnected from God? What did that season teach you?

3. Have you ever justified certain actions or decisions that, in hindsight, were rooted in ignorance rather than truth?

4. What does spiritual awareness mean to you now, and how has your understanding of "vanity" shifted over time?

5. Have you sensed an inner call to move beyond your current spiritual state? What might be holding you back from fully answering that call?

Chapter 2

THE UNSHAKABLE CALL OF GOD

"No one can come to me unless the Father who sent me draw him, and I will raise him on the last day."
John 6:44 (NABRE)

To have a true and complete relationship with God, you must answer the call of obedience. Before you've done so, there is often a yearning of this inner voice, quite difficult to ignore, which calls you to action. In Acts 9:15–18, when Saul was called, he had no choice but to answer. In Jonah 3:1–3, Jonah was called, and he indeed answered. I know you have your own experience of how you were called, and you answered. Maybe you are being called now but you are skeptical about it. Some people were called through others who answered the call earlier, while others were called through the inner voice or otherwise. No matter how you were called or are being called, the important thing is you cannot but yield to the call. This prevailing inner voice is a force "power." Since, this call is considered good, as you will know later, I as a pilgrim believed it was God the Almighty that beckoned for a transformation in my life.

A life in the Spirit is a life that shares a deep and unbarred relationship with Christ, the Holy Spirit, His angels, and His divinely begotten children. Christ said in the scripture that God is a spirit and those that worship Him must worship Him in Spirit and in truth. Also, Romans 8:1–17 indicates the need to live a life in the spirit. In Romans 8:9 (NABRE), it says: "But you are not in the flesh; on the contrary, you are in the spirit, if only the Spirit of God dwells in you. Whoever does not have the Spirit of Christ does not belong to Him."

The answer to this call was worthwhile and quite fulfilling to me. In this world, Paul was trying to explain in his letter to the Galatians 5:16 about the nature of life in the spirit as opposed to the nature of life in the flesh. All supposed efforts while living out life in the flesh turn to indebtedness. The flesh is a world of ignorance, a world without Christ. A life that does not give account to one's Maker. A period when one is advised to follow the guidance of the commandments or tenets of divine rules and regulation (which, by the way, give life), and so it would be rebuffed. This life of ignorance may appear attractive and indulgent but it profits absolutely nothing. It leaves one with regrets—if not immediate, then in the long run. Have you ever asked yourself, what is the use of this, in the end? Critical to note is that there is constant war between light (the new life in Christ, where we should be) and darkness (the dominion of Satan, where we should never be).

Like vanity, stains incurred from the other world are revealed. Thank God, who never abandoned this pilgrim. The precious blood of Jesus Christ is very efficacious at cleansing and removing these stains. Freedom can be gained from all manner of demeaning spiritual and physical chains. Like a small baby, everything becomes new when the Holy Spirit gets involved to help. How to speak, what to speak, which language to speak, meeting different people and how to mingle, etc., becomes your new world. Above all, how to experience the realness of God's existence will occupy your thought process. And just like Job 42:5–6 (NABRE) says, "I have heard of You by the hearing of the ear; But now my eye sees You; Therefore, I retract, and I repent, sitting on dust and ashes."

As a pilgrim, I did not only know about this God whom I was told about in the catechism of the Catholic Church and what the Bible said; I experienced God's nature personally. It was exposed to me how God operates, speaks, what He needed from me. I knew when He was offended; I understood how He chastises to reform His own; I learned how I would benefit, and what awaits those who remain faithful to the last. Indeed, it is a whole lot of experiences too numerous to mention.

In all this, God—Creator of Heaven and Earth, who is described in Isaiah 9:5 (NABRE) as: ". . . Wonder-Counselor, God-Hero, Father-Forever, Prince of Peace"—is, indeed, the Jireh, "provider." He is the Mighty God, the everlasting Father. He is the Good Shepherd. He is the I AM (always in existence), that is, being in the present. He is the Alpha (Beginning) and Omega (End). He is Rabboni (Master/Teacher). He is the Triumphant King of Ages, the Glorious God as was revealed in Mount Tabor during the Transfiguration. He is the Fourth Person in the Fire that Shadrach, Meshach and Abednego were thrown into. What do you call Him? For me, given how I have experienced Him, I call Him amongst other names my Ebenezer (my Stone of Help). My Baal-perazim (My Breakthrough God). The Lifter of my Head. Amazing Grace. Dear Beloved, God is indeed awesome.

He has a name for me as well. I am His White Lily. I am His Olaoma (Precious Pearl). Someone once told me that God was telling him about me and described me as a lioness (strong, fearless, and courageous). I have a passionate relationship with God, and we have an everlasting covenant. In this relationship,

I see myself as God's Precious Princess who has a special seat at the feet of her Maker. I took this seat more than twenty-six years ago during a time of very deep worship, when I became so overwhelmed by His glory and I saw myself embracing the feet of Christ where He sat on His throne. That was how I earned that spot.

At the beginning of my relationship with God, it was not so smooth. There was subtle childish opposition from me time and time again, and whenever I opposed His directive, I would lose my peace and get frustrated on that path. When I reflected on what could have led to the quagmire, I, like Jonah, realized that it was because I tried being stubborn or smart with God. The only option was to completely follow His instructions, and when I did, I had recovered my much-cherished peace, which led to achievement and my desired success.

I would remember clearly one of the times when I felt things did not go as smoothly as expected. I momentarily lost my peace. Then there came a time when some of my Christian brethren requested I follow them to visit an ailing sister. Out of frustration regarding my circumstance at that time, I declined abruptly to go with them. In that mood, I headed home. It was during my university days, and when I got to my room, I saw that a Christian sister of mine left a book on my reading table. This book was titled, *I Missed You*. I was a bit startled, wondering why such a sister would be reading a book captioned in this manner. After taking a second look and reading the part of the book that discussed the topic "I missed you," I saw that it talked about how God missed a Reverend Father who used to visit the Blessed Sacrament often, but when things became quite successful, the Father allowed his work to inhibit him from visiting the Blessed Sacrament for prayers, contrary to his usual practice. When this priest started reneging on visiting God's presence (before the Blessed Sacrament) as regularly as he used to, he started facing unusual challenges for which he could not immediately decipher the cause. He kept on managing his challenges until a day came that the priest was working on something, and an elderly woman came around. She told him that Christ said He missed him when the priest did not come to visit Him at the Blessed Sacrament. The priest immediately made amends and started visiting the Blessed Sacrament, and suddenly, just as was expected, one after the other, all those challenges he was facing vanished. So, this explained the caption "I missed you."

Having read this passage of the book, I asked a question, directing it to God in my mind. I said: "So how did this story affect me?" A voice within me said, "It affected you in the sense that presently, you are disenchanted and unhappy due to some unresolved issues that were disturbing you. These issues, because you were so concerned about them, created a barrier between yourself and God. Due to this barrier, whenever you pray and want to get to God, you can't gain access." I then asked, "What am I expected to do?" The spirit of God answered, "Ignore the difficulties as though not present and focus on absolutely praising God and attracting His presence." That when I do, the presence of God would overshadow me, and His glory would melt the problems away. This was a great eye-opener for me, as it really worked when I started putting it into practice. All those challenges I allowed to overwhelm me were taken away one after the other. Not only that, but my joy was also restored.

Another teaching from God I got was on handling the storms of life when they come my way. God once created a scenario of someone walking with an open umbrella during windy weather, and someone standing with an open umbrella during windy weather. He asked, "Of these two, which do you think would be easily swept by the wind?" I pondered a while and answered, "It would be the person who was walking with an umbrella wide open over the head." He said, "Correct, because the weight is firmer while standing than while walking. So," He advised, "when challenges rear up, you are not expected to be hysterical. Rather, stay calm, watch, pray before acting further." When this is done, it enables you to avoid being easily swayed by difficulties. When you are still (calm) in the face of challenges, you will receive the divine wisdom to handle that situation appropriately.

If you understand God, He speaks in various forms, but one or two of the ways to discern if He is the One speaking is His way of using the Scripture to support the message and situation. When He explained to me a scenario such as the one I mentioned above, He backed it up with the Holy Scripture in Matthew 7:24–27 (NABRE).

Another way of discerning when God speaks to you is checking if the conversation or information left you peaceful within.

I have been using some of the wise instructions that the Holy Spirit taught me on my journey as a pilgrim and they have all worked perfectly well. Though, as a human, sometimes I do forget and act by my own will. However, once I recall, I return to my divine manual.

There was a day (during my university days) when I met a Christian sister on her way to the private school hostel where I resided. She informed me of how depressed she was at that moment and was almost having suicidal thoughts. As she told me her ordeal, in a flash, my mind went to the story I had mentioned earlier in this book titled *I Missed You*. Then, I shared with her the whole story and how my challenge then was resolved. To the glory of God, I was amazed seeing this Christian sister of mine weeping on hearing this story, and she exclaimed. "Sister, you just saved my life. I feel so liberated on hearing this story." That is what the experience of the Word of God does. You get delivered from whatever would have locked you in beyond your control and against your will.

Another remarkable thing I learnt was when God said to me, "Gerardine, do you know, not all that glitters is gold?" He said

I should look at the palm of my hand, which had two sides—darkened and lightened sides. As I looked, I was asked, "Which of the two sides would you prefer?" I said the lightened side because it looked more beautiful and attractive. So, to you now, take a sincere quiz without spying on the explanation made for this: Which side of the palm of your hand would you like to pick and why?

The Holy Spirit (whom I referred to here as God) elucidated by saying, "Those two sides can be seen as the world of light and darkness, or what God gives and what Satan gives. He said: "When you pick the darkened side, which is the upper side of your palm, though it is initially unattractive, you would then walk into the brighter part of your palm, which is blissful. However, if you go first for the inner part of your palm, though it's brighter and attractive, you will come out through the darker part of your palm, which signifies misery, hardship, and discomfort."

I learnt so much with this. I understood that the journey with God as a pilgrim is a patient, deliberate, and consistent effort. It may sometimes appear not so palatable at the beginning. However, with sincerity of purpose and perseverance, you would eventually come out to the brighter side, where you would enjoy all you have desired and more. This experience, apart from being blissful, would also be permanent. Whereas, on the other hand, should one initially take the side of the palm that is so bright, so alluring, the experience would be ephemeral and eventually would lead to the darkened part of the palm, which would end with permanent torture, everlasting regrets, and damnation—God forbid! What a lesson. This to me is so big and quite deep. There is no better way to explain what life on Earth and beyond entails. God is love. Though He dwells in an unapproachable fire, He relates with His children with so much simplicity. What in-depth knowledge, a treasure of the divine! When you allow God to take you through the process, no matter how the journey is, He will teach you and reveal so many mysteries of life, just as He taught me and still does.

That is why, whenever I reflect on all that I have experienced in life, especially having known Him, I would say that this relationship I have shared with God as a pilgrim could only be called the awesomeness of God's grace. How can one express this enough, how amazing God's grace is, except to take a step of faith, answer the call as I did, and experience Him in fullness.

When you meditate on the importance of water to life, then you will understand better the experience of a priest who decided to relate his pilgrim experience by producing water, called Aqua Rapha. Even Christ acknowledged this of Himself when He said to the Samaritan woman: "If you knew the gift of God, and who it is who is saying to you, 'Give Me a drink,' you would have asked Him, and He would have given you living water" (John 4:10, NABRE).

I heard an inner voice, whom I believe was God, that once told me, "Out of your belly shall flow rivers of life-giving water" (John 7:38). This signifies eternal sustenance in God Almighty. That also means everything you need (I mean anything), you will get from your Creator and there will be no lack. Since this life-giving water is flowing from one's belly (you already know the importance of the belly), surely the flow shall get to others. Then, through you, they would be called to the banquet of the Lamb who is Christ the Lord and King.

I have been taught so many divine mysteries, songs, and dreams as I journey in this divine relationship. Some I will try to put in here to help in soul winning and soul building for God's kingdom.

Pause and Reflect

God calls each of us into a deeper relationship with Him, often in ways we least expect. Answering His call requires faith, surrender, and a willingness to step into the unknown. Just as many before us have wrestled with doubt before embracing His presence; we too must make the choice to listen, trust, and follow.

Take a moment to reflect on your personal journey. How has God been calling you? Are you fully listening, or are there fears and distractions holding you back?

Reflection Questions:

1. How did you first become aware of God's presence in your life?

2. Have you ever felt God calling you to something greater? How did you respond?

3. What obstacles have made it difficult for you to fully surrender to God's call?

4. How can you strengthen your ability to recognize and trust God's voice?

5. In what ways can you encourage others who may be hesitant to answer God's call?

Chapter 3

SIGNS AND WONDERS IN THE HEAVENS

"The heavens declare the glory of God; the firmament
proclaims the works of his hands."
Psalm 19:2 (NABRE)

One fateful day, on December 29, 2022, to be precise, I woke up in the morning to make breakfast and as I looked up at the clouds, I saw some beautiful but strange marks. Some of the marks were like steps beautifully arrayed with white clouds and other marks looked like an inverted V at the bottom of one line at the right-hand side. There was another long line which looked like a long X, and long lines like H. There were double paralleled slanted lines that went up and down. These signs were complex and boldly written. Due to my curiosity, I decided to check the cloud on the other side of the living room. To my amazement, these signs were seen on the other side of the living room too. This got me thinking, and I understood from that moment that the marks had meaning. It was God trying to speak to me.

The lines were long, bold, and persisted for a while. They later ceased appearing until about five months later, when I saw the steps in the clouds again with some of the lines drawn. These appeared some two miles away from my house, where I went grocery shopping. What made it strange was when I got to my house the same day, I noticed odd marks up in the clouds. I really knew God was speaking to me through these signs. I tried to make sense out of the strokes.

Before going into the interpretation of these strokes, I want to say how I knew God was speaking to me when I started getting visitations from several species of birds that came around my house at various intervals. Most prominent were the hummingbirds, cardinal birds, and the sparrows with different colors. One of the birds released feces right beside me. Then you could see some passing by my pathway sometimes, or flocking just two or three steps from where I had stood. There were some two birds that were visiting my window during half of the year with the same characteristics as the hummingbirds. They looked different though. It was the Holy Spirit that revealed to me their name: falcons. What astonished me was when I checked the name on Google search, the picture that appeared was exactly the type of birds that were visiting my room window. I equally observed how one day, as I stepped out of the house, I heard the strange noises of several birds but couldn't immediately sight them. Then suddenly appeared a black flock of birds, more than twenty-five in number, that flew past in the sky. They were close enough that I could see them very well, and they made loud noises as they flew. Just at the same time came flocks of white birds (very white) with about the same number, flying past as if they were chasing the black birds. So, the black birds flew to the left-hand side and the white birds flew ahead to the right-hand side. It was very strange as I pondered what that could be, yet I proceeded to where I was going.

These were occurrences that were not evident in my life prior to this time. The hummingbirds visited my window for months around a specific time of the day, usually in the mornings. During this period, I was quite weary and needed comfort, and God used these creatures to teach me that even the birds of the air did not sow or reap or store away in barns, and yet their heavenly Father fed them. Are you not worth more than sparrows? (See Matthew 6:25–34.) Glory to God! Indeed, like speed faster than flashes of light, God, day after day and one after another, eased those burdens that came my way, because of His mercy and grace. Whenever the signs appeared in the clouds—including double rainbow signs—specific matters that were hanging over me were resolved.

I had times when I bought crates of eggs and almost all of them had two egg yolks in one egg. When it seemed as if the era of double yolks was over, I bought another crate of eggs and some had double yolks again. So frightening, but real.

My research revealed that two (or more) egg yolks seldom occur. They may appear in one out of one thousand eggs. I can then imagine having such in all eggs in a crate. It could only be a bizarre miracle or strange mystery. When God decides to bless His own, He gives exponentially. I took pictures of these things and have copies of these photos. Indeed, I do testify that I am a living witness, just as it was indicated in an old hymn ("Trust and Obey"), which states: "When we walk in the Lord in the light of His word, what a glory He sheds on our way . . ."

I really have much knowledge of interpreted mysteries that I would want to share, but it may be overwhelming for one book. I will try to take it step by step and most likely put these mysteries into a series. However, some have been included in this book.

INTERPRETATION OF THE SIGNS I SAW IN THE SKY:

Back to the interpretations of the letters and lines I made out from the signs I saw in the sky.

The parallel lines: The two parallel lines up and down were likened to the link between Heaven and Earth, human and God. Parallel is an infinite line. That means God and human beings do have infinite covenants or relationships filled with love, blessings, protection, and life-giving knowledge. God through this sign was reminding me of my covenant with Him, which is eternal, one that is indivisible.

The sign that looked like big, bold X: X in Greek is Christ. X is also a mystery number in mathematics that one must find. I was reminded to look unto Christ my Author and Finisher all the days of my life. I know that alphabetically, X is number twenty-four. Twenty-four, I learnt, stands for priesthood. The number twenty-four signifies God's presence, rebirth, and blessings. The sign X also shows the four cardinal points (east, west, north, and south). This indicates that the whole universe wants to help throughout my lifetime. This would make sense to you also, once you believe this divine revelation. The sign X for me signifies the equilibrium stage of life, which enables an inevitable breakthrough. I witnessed this and can with every sense of responsibility attest to it. By X having four cardinal points, it also means air, water, fire and earth (the four elements of life—man relies on these elements to survive). So, GOD brought all these four elements together to be at peace with me, hence the liberation I experienced over my challenges. Alleluia!

The inverted big V sign found at the bottom of the X sign by the right-hand direction: The letter V is number twenty-two. The inverted shape looked triangular (two strokes meeting at a point). The symbol V signifies victory or peace and unity according to information from a Google search. It signifies honesty, reliability, efficiency, and focus. It represents teamwork. That is, working together with God and His Christ through the help of the Holy Spirit (the Tripartite God), coterminous with the tripartite being (mind, body, and soul). The number twenty-two signifies that things are happening in alignment with divine will for my life. Therefore, if you find a V significant to you or in your revelations, know that you are aligned and working or walking with the divine who is God. Finding the V sign at the end of one of the parallel lines by the right-hand side also indicated that God's love is infinite and He is present to connect me with His peace, which the world was not ready to give. Equally, it indicated that God has assured me victory.

The sign that looked like a big majuscule letter H that I saw in the sky: The letter H is number eight. It signifies a strong drive for success and a balance (H) symbol. It represents the notion of infinity, spiritual perfection, completeness, and purity. For Christians, the number eight represents the beginning of a new life and eternal life. The number eight is affirmation from the divine that one is destined for greatness.

Indeed, I have been inspired by God through the scriptures, by interpretation of mysteries, by dreams and revelations, and by day-to-day activities. I do not know that God exists just by what I was taught in the catechism of the Church or scriptural doctrines by priests of God and other evangelists; I have been convinced beyond doubt by my own vast experiences. So, these thoughts of mine are not mere imaginations or brainwashed teachings as some may assume. They are life realities, or what I will call the personal and practical encounters of my real-life experiences. This book is organic, a self-account of how I have been navigating my Christian life journey, as inspired by the Holy Spirit of God.

Pause and Reflect

Throughout history, God has used signs and wonders to reveal Himself to His people. Whether through nature, visions, or divine encounters, He speaks in ways that remind us of His presence, power, and purpose. Recognizing these signs requires a heart that is open and attentive to His voice.

As you reflect on this chapter, think about the ways God has revealed Himself in your life. Have you noticed His hand at work in unexpected ways? Are you paying attention to the signs He is placing before you?

Reflection Questions:

1. Have you ever experienced a moment where you felt God was revealing Himself to you through nature or a sign? What was it?

2. How do you discern whether something is a message from God or just a coincidence?

3. What biblical examples of God revealing Himself through signs inspire you the most?

4. How can you cultivate a heart that is more aware and receptive to God's messages?

5. In what ways can you encourage others to recognize and trust in God's presence in their lives?

Chapter 4

DELIVERANCE, DREAMS, AND REVEALED SONGS

"You are my shelter; you guard me from distress; with joyful shouts of deliverance you surround me."
Psalm 32:7 (NABRE)

I am compelled to share some experiences here in this chapter to indicate more ways God showed me He truly exists.

GOD DELIVERED ME—THE STORY OF A PACKET OF SALT WITH JESUS ON THE CROSS BENT TO HIS LEFT HAND:

This is a personal and victorious testimony. Some years back, immediately after marriage, the evil one afflicted me with a terrible moving object. This was accompanied by excruciating pain, a type better imagined than experienced. It was so discomforting that anytime this object moved and relaxed at a particular part of my body, it would pin that point down with severe pain as if that part of the body had been possessed. It was a terrible experience. I learnt evil people cast this as a spell. In addition, a familiar taximan once informed my elder sister and I that his family hurriedly ran away from a house because of the affliction his wife suffered. Apparently, he was reliably informed that their wicked landlady afflicted the wife with a worm-like moving object. He confessed that whenever his wife was confirmed pregnant, this evil worm would move vigorously to eat up the fetus and the wife would miscarry. However, after he sought help and left the evil house, his wife shortly got pregnant and had the baby. This was after being tormented by the evil object for more than ten years of marriage and living in the house of an evil landlady. Coincidentally, I once stayed in that house briefly. The taximan did not know I had the same issue. He was innocently informing us of what he suffered spiritually in his former evil landlady's house. Little did he know that God used him to confirm to me where what I was experiencing then in my body emanated. To the glory of God, he was giving testimony that the wife eventually got delivered and gave birth to a child—offspring they didn't have over their many years of living in evil, maggot-infested building.

Well, I eventually got delivered as well, but my account was different. In the bid to get an answer to my prayer, someone advised me to seek the help of a certain "man of God." I was not the type for such; however, after much persuasion, I gave in and went to the one I was told was a true man of God, and the man acclaimed the same. No doubt he noticed I was skeptical about him. So, in one of the prayer sessions, this man tried handing over to me a packet of salt. Mind you, I needed immediate spiritual deliverance from a tormenting moving evil object. When I looked at the packet of salt, I noticed that it had a picture of a cross with Jesus hanging on it, and his neck was turned to the left side instead of the right side. I refused to take the salt. This so-called man of God was infuriated. He claimed how sincere he was and started mentioning all the famous men of God who were using fake powers except him. His explanation was so detailed, however, I was not convinced. I refused to succumb to his gimmick. Thank God for the Catholic Church. I was groomed with strong Christian doctrines, and I really learnt well.

I also want to thank my late father, Sir Eugene Obiegbu KSJ. While he was on Earth, he never took us to any evil place to seek a solution. We watched him commit to the Catholic Church's ways of worship. He used often his Sunday missal, legion of Mary books, the Catholic hymn book, Sacred Heart prayer books, Novena to the nine choirs of angels, etc., and these acts of his influenced us positively towards God as we grew up. I was also able to pull myself out of the situation because some few years before my encounter with the so-called man of God, I attended a Church retreat and the officiating priest of God revealed as well as admonished on the need for children of God to beware of buying certain religious sacramentals circulating everywhere. The priest informed us that not all of them were good for use, because some had been produced by the occultic kingdom in order to possess unsuspecting children of God. He specifically mentioned that Jesus Christ died on the cross with His head bent to the right side of his hands and not the left. God bless the day I heard this truth. It was this truth that saved me.

Despite that, I was having excruciating pains due to a strange moving object and needed an immediate solution; I vehemently rejected the evil salt that came in the form of holy salt. That man, the so-called man of God, was so sad and disappointed by my refusal to accept his spiritual salt. So, he left my house. We never came across each other again. I encouraged myself that I would rather stay with the pain than take any evil form of solution. I assured myself that God would eventually heal me. So, one day, the Holy Spirit ministered to my spirit, "A Day will come when you will wonder where the moving object went, because it will have disappeared." So it came to pass that it vanished with time, miraculously. Glory to God!

Oh, the goodness of God is so enormous. Just taste and see and you will be overwhelmed with His goodness just as I am. It is due to these overflowing experiences that I want the world to be part of this true life story and journey which I've called the pilgrim's journey.

Let me share this old song with you. I heard this song in the spirit and woke up from sleep singing it. This song came at a very trying moment of my life, when I felt alone, betrayed, dejected, and dried up. I needed comfort. I remembered sometimes, I would say to God in the place of prayer amid tears, that He should just allow me to hold His legs with my head bent down. He would say to me, "You know what, I don't want to see these tears anymore," and I would say, "Okay, Father." Yet, in the place of prayer, when I remember either His Goodness or some of my overwhelming burden, I cry again. Being a faithful and loving father, he comes through with various songs to suit my wounded heart while telling me to hold my peace, for the storm is over.

The Song: "HIS EYE IS ON THE SPARROW" BY ETHEL WATERS – 1975 (PSALM 32:8)

A few days after hearing this song in my sleep, I physically saw flocks of sparrows in large numbers fly through the front of my house. Two days later, I received in the mailbox very important letters I was expecting in order to move forward in my life at that time. What an amazing God we serve!

I heard yet another song in my sleep. With this song, I felt God came down Himself, fought a battle for me on Earth, and went back again to His place of abode.

I heard this victory song:

"Ome n' uko, omenuko;
Dike Dike re re, Dike dike re re;
Onye nkwo abaa, Onye nkwo abaa;
Ihe imere n'ede ooo, ihe imere n'ede eee."

Meaning:

The One who comes through during lack and adversity;
The Victorious Warrior;
It is you I make bold to praise;
What you have done speaks overwhelmingly loudly.

Then I heard this song:

"Hakuna Matata, Hakuna Matata, Hakuna Matata, Hakuna Matataaaaa."

When I checked the meaning of the lyrics of the song, it implies that the troubles or problems are over (the storm is over).

In this trying period, God used so many songs—too many to write here—to talk to me about His unfailing love and care for me.

When you walk in His light (along with God), though sometimes trials may make you feel that God has abandoned you, no, He did not. When you feel low as you take your pilgrim's journey, never feel ashamed to tell it all to God, who really understands your situation and who will truly come through for you. One time, I broke down before my Creator. Why not?! Even Jesus Christ broke down at the Garden of Gethsemane when He cried to the Father to take away the cup, though not His will, but the will of God be done. On His way to the place of the skull for crucifixion, He fell thrice and got up. So, it is never wrong to be broken by the weight of life's burdens. What is bad is failing to tell it all to your Maker and failing to take His hand of help when He offers it. Let us learn from Peter. When Peter saw the wind, and he was afraid and beginning to sink, he cried out "Lord, save me!" Immediately, Jesus stretched out his hand and took hold of him and said to him, "You of little faith, why did you doubt?" (Matthew 14:30–31 NABRE). Peter took the hand, and he did not drown.

Let us remember that indeed Christ is our help and our light.

DREAM ABOUT THE INSCRIPTION, "CHRIST THE LORD IS KING":

In one of my dreams, I saw this inscription written boldly, and it magnified in the air and shifted around in the atmosphere intermittently. It stated: "CHRIST THE LORD IS KING." As I looked at it, someone like an elder called me by my name and asked, "Where is your sword?" I looked, but I was not with a physical sword. Then he opened a box like a mailbox and brought out a bunch of keys. He then said to look up. As I looked, I saw a church. He asked me to go in there and get something. I entered the church and the priest had just blessed a golden handkerchief that was shared with the congregation. I waited to get mine.

Something remarkable happened while I waited for the priest to enter the church so that I would enter. As the priest passed by, his white, priestly alb brushed against me and pulled the stone used to decorate my dress. As a result, the right-hand side of his alb got torn. He seemed not to have noticed it and proceeded inside the church. He celebrated the mass and left. I was so disturbed about what happened that I approached one of the mass servers to explain to him what had happened, and I apologized. When I woke up from the dream, I was so worried in real life. I wondered what the dream could mean, especially when I was asked where my sword was. Then, the tearing of the priest's alb that touched the stone used to decorate my dress. Someone tried to explain to me that the sword of the spirit means the Word of God. I also felt that the elder I saw in my dream who asked me about my sword was an indication that I was expected to carry along with me anywhere I went my God-given "symbol of authority." My sword should be my "office emblem" as a child of God, one who has been called for a special purpose. Another person explained that the tearing of part of the priest's wear when it touched me had to do with my call to prophetic ministry. Coincidentally, the priest I saw in this dream was a well-known and strong priest in a prophetic ministry.

It was ascertained (through this dream that Christ the Lord is King) that I have been called into the ministry of God's kingdom. Therefore, my sword should always be with me. Though the sword could mean the word of God, from my understanding, the sword here could mean my weapon—my symbol of authority as a child of God.

THE BURGER DREAM:

The burger as American cuisine is an "enduring icon." It symbolizes abundance, accessibility, and dominance.

On this fateful day, in the early morning of the day, I had a dream. I saw that I was with my son, who was seated while I stood to pick up a burger I had earlier ordered for and paid. However, I noticed many customers were being attended to, and they would leave. Those who ordered after me had their burgers and left while I was still waiting. I became agitated and started requesting that what I ordered should be given to me. A man who appeared to be one of the workers tried to calm me down, acting as if he wanted to solve the issue. Apparently, he did not. He merely listened to my complaint and left. Someone else was the one who came later and noticed that my tag number was placed deeper on the shelf, preventing my number from being picked up earlier. Some people who heard me complain had a surprised look on their faces as to why I was worried. That is how some human beings behave. Once an issue does not affect them, they do not care if you are unfairly treated. The joyous thing is that I finally got my burger.

The significance of this dream is, as I mentioned earlier, that the burger as American cuisine is an "enduring icon" which symbolizes abundance, accessibility, and dominance. As burgers represent abundance, the dream indicated that my ability to access the abundant blessing and possess it (the dominant aspect of having a burger) was being obstructed. This manifested in the form of the delay I encountered in getting my order prepared and delivered. How was this blessing delayed? It was because someone deliberately or mistakenly pushed my access number or tag deeper than necessary. It took the grace of God and deliberate prayers, as seen in my apprehensive manner in the dream, to attract a review and reconsideration. Then, I got my burger (now meaning blessings). Imagine that those who ordered burgers after me had theirs and left while I was still queuing in the line with no solution in sight—until I protested about the unfairness. Child of God, you have no reason to be silent in the face of adversity. I am glad I didn't keep quiet, so I was able to receive the **burger** I ordered and that became my **God-given abundance**, **accessibility**, and **dominance**!

Join me in prayer if you want to experience this God. Sing and meditate along with me. This song is one of my favorites from the *Ancient and Modern Hymn Book* we used to sing years back, during my secondary school assembly/morning devotion.

It is titled: "My God, How Wonderful Thou Art, Thy Majesty How Bright," by Frederick William Faber (1848).

PRAYER:

"My God and Father, you are the Almighty. Beside You there is no other God. You Created man in Your image and likeness so that You will be worshipped and praised but man has failed in many ways to keep this precept. Please, accept me the way I am now and draw me back to yourself for I am truly sorry for all my sins. Forgive me and fill me with Your amazing grace so that I will be whole again to experience the power and joy of Your salvation. Thank You for answering my prayer through Jesus Christ our Lord, Amen.

Pause and Reflect

God speaks to His people in many ways—through deliverance, dreams, and even songs. These divine encounters remind us that He is always present, guiding, protecting, and revealing His will. Sometimes, the answers we seek come through visions in the night or melodies that stir our spirits. Recognizing and embracing these moments deepens our faith and trust in Him.

As you reflect on this chapter, consider how God has spoken to you. Have you experienced His guidance in unexpected ways? How can you become more attuned to His voice in your daily life?

Reflection Questions:

1. Have you ever experienced a dream or vision that you felt was from God? What message did it convey?

2. How has God used music or songs to speak to you or bring comfort in difficult times?

3. In what ways have you seen or experienced deliverance in your life?

4. How can you become more aware of the different ways God communicates with you?

5. What steps can you take to strengthen your faith and trust in God's divine guidance?

Chapter 5

THE FLOW OF
AMAZING GRACE

---

*"But He said to me, 'my grace is sufficient for you, for
power is made perfect in weakness.' I will rather boast
most gladly of my weaknesses, in order that the power
of Christ may dwell with me."*
2 Corinthians 12:9 (NABRE)

God is love. He is overwhelmingly awesome. In Romans 5:6 (NABRE), it says, "For Christ, while we were still helpless, yet died at the appointed time for the ungodly." The scripture further says what greater love is this that a man laid down his life for another.

Picture Christ in a moment on the cross where He was crucified. You will see that even there, His amazing grace flowed in the form of blood and water. When the blood touched the earth, there surely was a reaction. At His passing on the cross, the centurion soldier exclaimed that truly this is the son of God. Equally, there was an account of an earthquake, in which some who were dead centuries ago rose to life. What an amazing display of grace. The impact then up to the present brings rebirth, which is amazing and impactful. The awesomeness of God's love was exhibited again on the cross when Jesus told the robber crucified at His right side: "Amen, I say to you, today you will be with me in Paradise" (Luke 23 verse 43). This was simply because the thief asked Christ to remember him in His kingdom. In other words, he meant, please let Your grace flow within and over me. Of course, the grace had to flow on even the robber because he asked with a sincere and committed heart. Christ being who He is, One who promises and never fails, willingly released His saving grace.

I experienced personally this grace of God. It flowed when I simply asked of Him, "Yes Lord, I do not know how to pray—teach me how to pray." He released His grace on me, and my life became renewed. From that moment in 1995, I craved to be in His presence. I do experience the flow of His presence whenever I stay conscious of Him. I pray and see the request granted instantly, to my bewilderment yet great admiration. This spurs my zeal in fellowshipping with God. Material things don't really matter to me anymore. For instance, while in the university, my studies were controlled by Him. My efforts were strongly influenced by the Holy Spirit. He inspired my writing using available knowledge within me and expanded it so much that when I did my mini-projects (term paper assignments), both my lecturers and the person who typed my academic works would express surprise. To them, they wondered how someone with my level of education (as an undergraduate then) and age could write so well. For instance, the university typist once said, "Whenever I read your mini-projects, I wonder and thrill at the level of intelligence you exhibit in your writings. Among all the students I type for, I love reading your term papers. You are so conscientious."

In another instance, while going through my mini-project during my 100 level (first year in the university as an undergraduate), my Sociology lecturer (a professor and PhD holder) asked if I was truly the one who wrote the term paper assignment I submitted. I said I wrote the work wholly by myself, backed with research that I was expected to do. I told him that indeed, I wrote the assignment all through the night. Truly that was so. I always do my write-ups all by myself and with the help of the Holy Spirit, who often inspired me with deep teachings beyond the classroom knowledge. This explained why I was always among the best academically at any level of studies I had ever undertaken—primary to tertiary levels. My professional career development and workplaces are not exempted. Some people have said my brain is not of this world, and I believe them because I do wonder sometimes; it could only be divine that I could be inspired to say or write certain things. Most times, I have learnt from what I said or wrote. I only ascribe this to the grace of God through His Holy Spirit.

This amazing grace of God is like refreshing water from a cistern. I remember vividly one of the periods during my final year university examination when I had so much information I needed to acquire for my last examination in the university. When I couldn't physically cope to cover the necessary reading, the Holy Spirit said to me: "Ensure your eyes go through all the words of the book. Just scan the book with your eyes." It looked stupid and could not immediately make sense. How would I just scan words with my eyes without bothering to understand? Yes, I was so tired that I couldn't read further, let alone bother to understand. However, as irrational as that instruction seemed, I fully obeyed. On the examination day for that course, as the examination answer sheets were shared, I heard in my mind, "Pick up your pen and write." Indeed, after a short prayer, I picked up my pen and wrote all the thoughts that were within me. These thoughts were flowing like a river and never stopped. I wrote and covered the first examination answer sheets and called for extra answer sheets. Grace indeed speaks! Though my human strength almost failed me during the preparation for final year university examination, God's grace came through for me to finish up. I came out with flying colors. I got all my final year subjects with As. This meant that I achieved grades rated 80% and above in all the courses I took.

Indeed, at this stage of my life, I speak what I know about God, and not only what I was taught about God. God is real and his amazing grace is indeed awesome!

This amazing grace is the divine oil that lubricates your relationship with God to make it seamless. It helps you to follow God naturally, not under compulsion. He really carried me on His wings, because under a transformed state, I operated by His inspiration and guidance. This caused me to have excellent results both in my studies and spiritual life.

Under God's amazing grace, just like me, you can operate in the realm of the Spirit to liberate those in captivity, and testimonies will abound to the glory of God. A schoolmate of mine, on the feast of Christ the King (this is a Catholic Church event that commemorates Christ's triumphal entry into Jerusalem shortly before the Passover feast), suddenly started laughing while we were on Procession. I inquired why and she said, "The way you take authority in the Spirit is overwhelming." I asked, "How?!" I knew she had a gift of visions—she could see things whenever prayer was going on. She further explained that whenever we prayed, and I made a decree, she could see all the strange spirits halt or scamper instantly. I smiled. That was grace and authority as a child of God, in action to the glory of God. You can experience it. It is given by God to His children freely. That is why it is said in Isaiah 55:1 (NABRE) "All you who are thirsty, come to the water! You who have no money, come, buy grain and eat; Come, buy grain without money, wine and milk without cost!"

It says also in Luke 4:18–19 (NABRE) that "the Spirit of the Lord is upon me, because He has anointed me to bring glad tidings to the poor. He has sent me to proclaim liberty to captives and recovery of sight to the blind, to let the oppressed go free, and to proclaim a year acceptable to the Lord."

The joy of this experience is that the flow of His grace puts you in an unimaginably comfortable and courageous state. People, powers, and animals will recognize that the seal of God is upon you. What an amazing experience God's grace bestows upon us.

Peter, while on his own pilgrim journey on Earth, was able to walk on the sea. At the beautiful gate in Acts of the Apostles, Peter said to the lame man who was begging that silver or gold he had none but in the name of Christ, he should stand up and walk. This happened just as Peter commanded. On the day when the Holy Spirit descended on him and the other disciples, Peter proclaimed the good news of Christ, and it was recorded that 3,000 men repented and followed the teachings of Christ, which centered on love for God and humanity.

When you allow this grace to dwell in you and flow through you, you will testify to God's goodness. Equally, you will become a divine source God uses to attract men into the amazing grace experience. I was attracted to it as I watched others, and so many have, through me, been drawn to this amazing grace experience. Another instance was captured in the Scripture in John 1 verses 43 to 51. This was the account of how Christ in Galilee found Philip and Peter, called them, and they became His disciples. Then as Philip experienced Christ's presence, he could not hold the joy of the experience to himself, so he went to call Nathanael to become a disciple of Christ. Nathanael hesitated, but Philip was not ready to let go. He said further, in verse 46 of John Chapter 1, "Come and see." That is what happens when you receive the grace of God. You are excited in such a way that you want to let everyone know and experience the same thing, especially your loved ones. Yes, Nathanael answered that call. He went to meet Christ and just as God gave freely His grace, Nathanael after his encounter with Christ exclaimed in John 1:49 (NABRE), "Rabbi, you are the Son of God; You are the King of Israel."

A vital thing to note should always be how to stay focused despite all these awesome experiences. The watchword is to stay undaunted, committed, and focused on the One who has called you to discipleship—who is Christ the King. There is a saying in my native language which literally means in English, "When a lizard removes its hand from a tree, surely the lizard would be caught." Peter walked on the sea when he focused on Jesus the Master, but when he realized what was happening, his focus changed, then he started drowning.

It is pertinent to note that this grace of God is fragile, sensitive like any other precious gift. When handled with care, it will ooze sweet aura all the way, but if it is uncared for at any point, just like a flood, it may flow away, and the receiver would become vulnerable to the storms of life. These storms could rage fiercely and become quite destructive. However, be aware that at any point in your life when the storms of this world come blowing to disrupt your peaceful existence, for whatever reason that they arose, you must reach out urgently to the Rabboni—Jesus the Christ and Master. Endeavor to seek Him to calm the troubled storm as He did in Mark Chapter 4 verses 37, 39, and 41.

God's grace ensures strength and beauty. It is likened to the bliss of heaven and must not be treated with levity. No wonder Eli the priest of God in the Scripture on hearing the death of his sons managed to hold on, but when he heard that the ark of the covenant had been captured by the Philistines, he collapsed and died (1 Samuel 4:18). Therefore, an Ichabod (without glory) situation must not be permitted and the glory of God that generates grace must not depart. It is indeed sacrosanct that you would live a conscious life in which God's amazing grace thrives.

I believe that living in God's grace, manifested by His glory, signifies being alive. When this experience is lacking, such a person might appear living but truly be dead.

In Psalm 51:12 (NABRE), David says: "Lord, restore to me the joy of your salvation; and uphold me with a willing spirit."

You may say this prayer: *"O God, let me be filled with Your Shekinah, glory, and may your grace overflow in my life. Amen."*

Pause and Reflect

God's grace is a limitless, unmerited gift that flows abundantly into our lives. It strengthens us in weakness, sustains us in trials, and lifts us when we fall. His grace is not something we can earn—it is freely given, a testament to His infinite love and mercy.

As you reflect on this chapter, consider how God's grace has shown up in your life. Have you fully embraced His unmerited favor, or are there areas where you struggle to receive it?

Reflection Questions:

1. When have you experienced God's grace in a way that left a lasting impact on your life?

2. How does understanding God's grace change the way you view your struggles and failures?

3. In what ways can you extend grace to others as God has extended it to you?

4. Are there areas of your life where you struggle to accept God's grace? How can you surrender them to Him?

5. How can you cultivate a daily awareness of God's grace and live in gratitude for His blessings?

Chapter 6

WALKING THROUGH THE VALLEY

"Even though I walk through the valley of the shadow of death, I will fear no evil, for you are with me; your rod and your staff comfort me." Psalm 23:4 (NABRE)

Beloved, in your journey as a pilgrim on earth, beware of the devil's porridge. Things that defile your soul or spiritual well-being, and even things that affect your physical wellness, may come in disguised patterns. Not everything that seems okay for your physical gratification is truly healthy. So, look out for such things to avoid them. Apostle Paul in his book to the Galatians in Chapter 5 verses 19–21 (NABRE) called these things acts of the flesh, and in verse 21, he said: ". . . I warn you, as I warned you before, that those who do such things will not inherit the Kingdom of God." If you keep going and thinking all is well, without being sensitive to the physical and spiritual happenings around you, by the time you see the devil's porridge, you will liken it to normal porridge. When you eat it, it will appear harmless; then it will overwhelm you and result in regrets and woes. You may imagine how harmless it is, not knowing that it would become a terrible thorn in your flesh and spirit.

Imagine for a few seconds how the devil tempted Eve in the story of the Garden of Eden, in Genesis 3 verses 1–19 (NABRE) with emphasis on verses 1, 4, 5, 6 ,and 13. I will pick up some of the words used: "Did God really say, you shall not eat from any of the trees in the garden?" The devil engaged as if he was harmless and had come in peace. Then, Eve gave the devil the total rundown of what they were required to do. Now having been equipped with more information, the devil acted again as a "caring" being and said in verse 4: "You certainly will not die!" However, by the time you finish reading the chapter, you will see that in verse 19, God was angry that they disobeyed His instruction and passed His punishment on them. Amongst other lines, God said to Adam: ". . . for dust you are and to dust you shall return." Remember that it was the devil who seduced the heart of the woman to make her consider the fruit beautiful and good for eating. Then she fell to the subtle seductive technique of Satan, and she ate the forbidden fruit and gave the same to Adam, her husband.

This seemingly innocent act at the beginning eventually made them lose their beautiful abode, bringing curses and death. Remember that the devil assured Eve that there would be no death but rather highlighted how knowledgeable they would become should they eat the forbidden fruit. The devil never allowed her to see that she was about to disobey God her Creator. The picture presented to Eve was only how useful eating the fruit would make them become. The devil always wants to get all the information about you and never wants you to know the consequence of any action you are subtly deceived to embark on.

What a liar! What a deceitful being! What a robber! What a destiny twister! What a destroyer! Please do everything possible to flee from the devil's promises. In other words, *beware of the devil's porridge.* Little by little, the enemy will engage you and lure you into a ditch. Hopefully, God will help you to come out alive. Many have not been so fortunate. The temptation that I referred to here as devil's porridge often appears simple at the start, easy, fascinating, and most times looks like the original, but it is not. This is a trick, a trap, a travesty. That is the reason the Bible says in 1 Peter 5:8 (NABRE): "Be sober and vigilant. Your opponent the devil is prowling around like a lion looking for someone to devour."

Having discovered that the Christian pilgrims know he roars, he now operates mostly in a subtle and swift way. Every Christian *must watch and pray.* This should be every Christian watchword: *watch and pray.*

As a pilgrim, though, still matching on, I had my own excruciating experiences. Be aware that the devil does not really come looking like a devil. You would see this in fellow human beings you deal with day by day. Some pop up suddenly while some may be members of your household, community, you name it. Since you may not really know the pattern or angle that could be used to offer you the abominable porridge, your ability to be alert and discerning in line with the words of God in the Scripture is very important. Equally, the sense of good logic or morals, of course, with the help of the Holy Spirit, cannot be over emphasized. As you journey along the route to the kingdom of God where Christ is the king, ask for the gift of wisdom and discernment. This will help you to identify what is truly good and bad in order to overcome it.

The overflowing grace God bestowed on me to express my zeal for His kingdom led to some of the things I already expressed in Chapter 3 of this book. Most of those beautiful experiences happened as victory over challenges caused by the devil.

As a pilgrim on the Christian journey, I surely had my own terrible and faith-shaking trials. I learnt when I fell that like Jesus, I had to rise and continue to look up to the finishing line. It is for me a journey of no retreat and no surrender. Thus, I decided to share in this book what I called wilderness experience and other short messages, such as the faithfulness of God; the power of God's love; some songs of praise to God whose lyrics addressed directly God as my Deliverer. These different past difficult moments and experiences were what I considered to be the crossroads/conditions that were low moments of my life. How God came through to deliver me, therefore, informed this chapter and other topics I had preached about at different fora. Incorporated as well is a topic that illustrates the grace derived as Christian pilgrims when we implore the intercession of Blessed Mother Mary.

In fact, I regard low moments of one's life as spiritual stagnancy. When I experienced my low moments, it was a period of dryness. A period I assumed I was abandoned by God and felt alone. It happened when I was fixing things by myself because I was impatient. I realized that all the times I went at my own pace, I suffered injuries, regrets, and further dryness.

When you accept to walk with God on this journey, always wait and make sure He is with you. If you are not sure, it would be better if you wait until you get clarity. No matter how long or short the wait, the clarity comes when we are patient. At times, it may look like God is silent, He somehow wants to teach us something, or He is waiting for an auspicious time. But as is often the case with human beings, we say nature abhors vacuums and we try to fill them. Hence, we end up with sad stories or memories.

Take, for instance, Moses—he understood the need to go with God so much that when God asked the Israelites to move because they had dwelt enough at a particular point, Moses hesitated but kindly put it: "If Your presence does not go with us, do not send us up from here." Exodus 33 verses 1, 2, 3, and 15 (NABRE). What a great move by a man called Moses, a great leader of the people while being an excellent and ardent follower of God.

It is pertinent to know that whatever happens is for a purpose. The ability to make amends when one navigates wrongly by not waiting for guidance is essential. Return, surrender, ask for pardon, and still wait to have that essential divine guidance. God will surely speak, so relax and listen in order to understand when He does. God speaks to us through our inner mind, through fellow Christian pilgrims who are at our level, or through elders in the Christian race. He also speaks through revelations and dreams; however, all words and teachings must be based on the already existing words of God as written in the Bible. At various stages of every trial, there are lots of things to learn. In the usual parlance at the workplace, it is said, "experience is the best teacher." So, in the Christian journey, I have to say, trials and persecutions generate the experiences that are used to get to the main destination, which is the kingdom of God and His Christ.

The experiences I have garnered, both the good and the very tough/unpleasant, have all properly equipped me. They have really fortified me to keep facing the challenges of life, hence, I am able to convincingly attest to what the Christian journey or walking with God entails.

Pause and Reflect

Difficult seasons are an inevitable part of life. These low moments may bring pain, doubt, and uncertainty, yet they also offer opportunities for growth, faith, and dependence on God. It is in these valleys that we come to truly understand His presence and strength.

As you reflect on this chapter, consider how your low moments have shaped you. Have they drawn you closer to God, or have they made you question His presence? How can you trust that He is walking with you, even in the darkest times?

Reflection Questions:

1. What has been one of the most challenging seasons of your life, and how did you see God working through it?

2. How do you typically respond to difficulties—do you turn to God or try to handle things on your own?

3. What lessons have you learned from past struggles that have strengthened your faith?

4. How can you shift your perspective to see challenges as opportunities for spiritual growth?

5. What scriptures or prayers bring you comfort when you are going through difficult times?

Chapter 7

TESTIMONIES, TEACHINGS, AND WORDS OF WISDOM

"Come and hear, all you who fear God, while I recount what has been done for me." Psalm 66:16 (NABRE)

---

*I*n this chapter, I have incorporated some of my personal encounters with divine occurrence, some bible stories, and inspiring words of wisdom. They are meant to enlighten people in a special way and reawaken souls for God who is the Creator.

ACCOUNT ONE: My personal story regarding my university admission, which indicated that God still works outstanding miracles in this age

Some years ago, I went to a place called Ikoyi in Nigeria, at the Joint Admission and Matriculations Board (JAMB) office to submit a JAMB form for another academic year. I did submit the JAMB form, but on leaving the premises, just at the gate I saw numerous people in the queue seeking to know if they were accepted into university. I was not expecting to have gained admission myself, since my earlier application seemed unsuccessful. As I was about to leave the JAMB premises, a voice within me requested I should enquire from the gateman whether I was granted admission into the university. I hesitated and decided to ignore the voice. But I had to succumb because the force within me was enormous. I obliged and requested the gateman to check if I was granted admission. True to the inner voice, which I understood was the Holy Spirit, the gateman in a few minutes returned to me with the news that I was given admission to study philosophy at Imo State University. Yes, the gateman was an angel in disguise. He requested I go to the distribution room in order to check if my admission letter was still available or if it might have been mailed to my address.

To my amazement, when I got to the distribution room, my admission letter was right there waiting for me to pick up. God indeed came through for me. Remember, I had already lost hope of getting admission into the university that year. That was why I bought a new JAMB form and went to the JAMB office to submit the form. However, God—who never says it is over until it is indeed over—planned a divine twist. A further twist happened when I reported to the university and made a request for change of course. The university granted me a change of course to study History and International Relations. I prayed to God for a miracle to study my dream course, which was Government and Public Administration. Yes, God truly answered the prayer. As the last lists of admission for the year were published in school, my name appeared on the list to study Government and Public Administration. Up till this day, nobody claimed to be the one who changed my admission. It was God all the way.

This story should be an encouragement to those who may want to give up on something good they most earnestly desire in life. Know that God sees and knows how best to fix your problems, and when He does, it is always unique.

Sing along as you read the next account.

"When I come into your presence, I'm so happy; When I come into your presence, I'm so glad; In your presence, there's anointing, and the Spirit moves around me; In your presence, anointing breaks the yoke." (Song writer: Unknown)

ACCOUNT TWO: Matthew 17:24–27, the story of money found in the mouth of a fish

In this account, there was a question raised by collectors of the two-drachma temple tax to Peter whether Jesus would pay the temple tax.

To show that Jesus abided by the law and had control over the universe, Jesus requested Peter to go to the lake, open the mouth of the first fish he caught, and take out "four-drachma coin" for the payment of His tax and the disciples.

Just as Jesus directed, so did it come to pass that a fish inside a sea conveyed the required currency and Peter used it to attend to that need.

The significance of this story is that God and His Christ have power to do all things and can call up treasures to meet the needs of those who believe in Him.

ACCOUNT THREE: Cast your net into the sea, Luke 5:4

In this account, the disciples of Jesus toiled all night for fish, being fishermen, but they could not catch any. However, when the master Himself (Jesus Christ) came, He asked them to cast their net deep into the sea, and behold, it was recorded that their story changed from not catching any fish to having so many fish in the net.

This explains that at every step of the way, despite the difficulties that may arise, the Master of the pilgrims, who is Jesus Christ, will make a way even where there seems to be none. The disciples in this account gave up, got frustrated. However, hope was restored at last.

During this pilgrim's journey hitherto, there have been all sorts of obstacles (physical and spiritual ones), but the One who has called me is faithful. He has been pulling me through. I had several occasions when I was at a crossroads, how to take the right step became vague, and suddenly the Helper (Christ) came to make it all well.

During examination periods at school, at times, He transports me into a realm where I carry out my tests seamlessly in a strange and miraculous way, especially when I most need God's intervention. The big question should be: Where did the fish go that the disciples of Jesus were not able to catch any all through the night? And where did the fish come out from within a split second? Little wonder the psalmist said "the earth is the Lord's and all it contains, the world, and those who dwell in it. For He has founded it upon the seas and established it upon the rivers." Psalm 24:1–2 (NABRE).

ACCOUNT FOUR: GENOTYPE SS CHANGED TO AA

A fellow pilgrim testified that his experience of what God does was so overwhelming that he once prayed for someone whose SS genotype (genetic makeup associated with sickle cell anemia) changed to AA. This was medically confirmed by a renowned government hospital.

Another fellow pilgrim was once shot at a university during her undergraduate days but because she was pleading the precious blood of Jesus Christ, the bullet could not penetrate her body. The robbers later slammed the knife at her back, but she was not hurt. This happened at a female-only hostel. This was the story of a Christian sister who suddenly appeared at the hostel after leaving school, where she went to read (night reading/class, as students often called it). However, unknown to her, robbers were raiding her fellow students in that hostel. Due to her sudden appearance and her consistent screaming about the precious blood of Jesus Christ having seen the terrible thing that was going on, the robbers hurriedly ran away. They could not bring her down because of the fire of God that was evident in her.

God used her to save other students who probably could have been raped, but her appearance in the middle of that night averted further damage. God is all powerful and rescues those who diligently follow Him whenever they are in trouble. Glory to God! Alleluia!

There are testimonies too numerous to recount. However, the few mentioned here are to demonstrate that all Christian pilgrims will be well protected. No matter how smooth or bumpy the road may be, there is the assurance that such a person will *never* be alone or abandoned by God. You will always emerge victorious.

WORDS OF WISDOM FROM THE AUTHOR

The conscience is every person's moral sense of right and wrong; the still small voice that assesses our actions and stirs us to act in certain ways. Most times, we silence and resist it. However, when we allow it to fully take charge as our official guide, we enjoy tremendous peace. When we ignore it, we lose our peace. There is an Igbo adage that says: "as you point one finger to someone, the other four fingers are pointing at you." Let us re-examine ourselves in all honesty, and maybe we can remedy the "self" in us. The best gift to give oneself is to be honest with oneself. Let us keep our conscience alive as we deal with each other. With the conscience fully active in a person's life, justice becomes a sine qua non.

God is still in the business of granting mercy and protecting His own. He has won all our battles ahead of time if we believe. I do believe. Remember, "some rely on chariots, others on horses, but we put our trust in the name of the Lord our God. They collapse and fall, but we stand strong and firm." Psalm 20:8–9 (NABRE). I don't know what your mind is saying but mine says, be still and you will see the wonders of God.

For instance, under the watch of Eli, the glory of God departed from among the Israelites. The ark of the covenant was taken away during a battle that saw the Israelites abysmally defeated. The focus here for me is "under the watch of Eli—a priest and leader of the people of Israel." Eli, on hearing that the ark of the covenant which carried God's presence had been snatched, was deeply grieved and he died instantly. Two things to take away:

1. Eli was a man of God, God's mouthpiece, but he refused to stand up against evil, even against abominations perpetuated in God's House, where he was a shepherd. He refused to be guided judiciously by his conscience in discharging his priestly duties.

2. Eli was afraid how his sons who submerged themselves in sin would feel should he stand his ground in guiding them right. They did everything that violated God's ordinances. He looked the other way as if nothing was wrong.

Are you trapped in this kind of situation? You, a man of God, you, a child of the Almighty God, have you refused to stand by God's standards for any reason? Fear the impending anger of God and amend your ways!

On my pilgrim's journey, as one called to follow the Son who is Christ, and as a Catholic, I have recourse to the Blessed Virgin Mary to assist me because sometimes the trials may be overwhelming. It is imperative to implore the help of the Holy

Spirit. Equally, the Holy Angels should be called upon to assist as one journeys through life, because God has commanded them to guide us not to stumble.

Regarding the Holy Mother Mary, for instance, she was the first to have deliberately evangelized me, as I indicated at the beginning of this book. She did this by ministering to my inner being to follow the Son, Jesus Christ. Just as in the Bible at the wedding in Cana, she said, "Do whatever He asks you to do." At first, I ignored the voice, but she did not relent. I then said if I excelled in all the subjects I wanted at the Senior Secondary School Certificate Level, then I will follow her son. I said this casually and never knew she took up the matter to resolve it, as she always has been known to do for those who have recourse to her. I did pass all the subjects, miraculously, exactly as I wanted. Then with the same voice, the Blessed Virgin Mary spoke again to me, saying: "I have done what you wanted; I want you to follow my son." I was reminded of my promise. Yes, I indeed remembered my promise and the zeal to follow Jesus Christ became dominant in me. I also felt it was honorable to fulfill my promise, having been granted my request. The encounter may appear strange or hard to believe, but with every sense of responsibility, I testify to this as the truth.

As I succumbed to the invitation to follow Jesus Christ, I started the journey of learning how to be a true and gallant follower. This has taken me through various stages of learning in the divine school of God and His Christ where the Holy Spirit of God is the Prefect and God in Action. I have over these several years acquired great organic wisdom—that is, the Holy Spirit of God has taught me so many things that were novel.

I have shared these teachings freely as well to some of my fellow Christians in my capacity as an evangelizer of the Gospel of Christ and prayer minister/leader. In their excitement, some have said things like: "Please keep teaching us, we love to listen and hear about your teachings, especially when you speak about Blessed Mother Mary." A particular woman said: "I have heard preaching on Mary but the dimension you gave about why Blessed Virgin Mary was called Virgin Most Prudent was so revealing and I have really learnt new things." After preaching on the faithfulness of God, someone said to me: "You are indeed an old soldier, because your preaching was quite original and as usual, very impactful." On another occasion, after teaching on wisdom, a Christian sister who benefitted from the lessons sent me a private message. In the message, she expressed how excited she was to have learnt very useful tips about wisdom. She then encouraged me to think about putting most of my teachings into book form so that more people will come to deeper knowledge of the things of God.

In her words, I quote: "Sister, have you thought about writing a book, or are you writing one? I have gone through your write-ups on wisdom severally and I gained wisdom. All these write-ups can become a book. What do you think? Remain blessed." There were instances when I prayed in public at various times and occasions to the glory of God. I had some people come to me and say: "The Holy Rosary you led was so strong." Another was: "After you prayed, when I got home, I wept, repented of my sins, and asked God to renew me." Another said: "When you were praying, it was as if you should not stop because Heaven opened." A Christian sister was so excited to testify that a serious medical condition in her brother's life got an instant turnaround after I mentioned the case in a prayer session. In some of her words: "Sis. Gera., my sister, joined me to praise God because He has done me well . . . God that uses you to do wonders, God that delivers through you, your word of prayer, the words that come out of your mouth have fire. I pray that God will continually let His light shine on you. Thank you for what you are doing for the kingdom. Thank you and God bless."

There was a situation where a certain general manager at my previous workplace insisted that I should be sought to pray during a birthday event organized for him at work. Others volunteered to pray but he insisted that they should "call Gerardine to come and pray." I have heard a report referring to me, where someone said: "Since she prayed that prayer in Jerusalem and people were falling to the ground due to the presence of the Holy Spirit, I became afraid of her." Even at a certain time in a dream, I saw a short demon who, on sighting me, screamed and ran back, shouting, "You are a special child of God, you are from God." These are just a few comments from various people who benefitted from God's benevolence through me. These comments are not in any way meant to attract undue attention but to glorify God that He is all powerful, wisdom personified, and His spirit is active and alive eternally. I have always acknowledged that it has been God all the way. After all, He once told me: "Gerardine, you do not know how to pray. Tell God to teach you how to pray." When I said yes, I do not know how to pray, God taught me how. Instantly, my tongue twisted and muttered things I didn't quite understand.

I later got to know when I started growing more in Christ that the tongue twist I experienced and the strange language was spiritual language (praying in tongues). Till today, I do not use my own words to pray. Rather, I pray based on what I hear and what God puts in my mind. It is not surprising, therefore, that it has been widely noticed that I pray differently. Someone would call me "my great intercessor." Various persons have equally informed me of what they have seen around me, some during prayers. Someone saw a gigantic Holy Angel behind me. Another saw moving stars all around me with the inscription: "do not touch." Another saw fire in my hands. Another said: "Your eyes are terrifying, do not look at me." There was one who said: "Gallant child of God who has the gift of speaking in tongues that releases fire."

My elder sister would sometimes with excitement on sighting me exclaim: "The Angelic Voice." Indeed, I know that these various reports are true of me to the glory of God. Equally, the non-Christians I have had the opportunity to interact with during some of my Christian ministerial activities or at other professional levels have benefitted from this wealth of wisdom and God's abiding presence. There has been instant deliverance, healing, and restoration in other specific cases after I prayed in such a way that left me bewildered. I am now inspired to also mention these cases briefly. A case of several years of excruciating hemorrhage/pile was instantly cured. A heavy abscess scheduled for operation got busted in a few minutes after I prayed. Healing took place and the operation was canceled because the patient received divine and instant healing. Acute fever disappeared, and so many others. May God alone be glorified. God is real!

I was advised by wisdom in the early stages of my Christian life that I did not need to do so much in seeking the wealth of this world, but I should faithfully follow God and He would take care of my needs. Surely there have been bumpy times, but as the calmer of the storm, Christ has readily waded the storm and ensured deliverance, freedom, and prosperity. An attempt will convince you.

I am convinced that with God, there will always be something remaining. The flour never finishes, nor will the oil run out. There will always be that remaining thing in your hand to part your Red Sea for a thoroughfare. There will always be that little child to bring the five loaves of bread and two fishes to satisfy your hunger and revive your weary soul. Do not give up—there is still the third day for the resurrection, and you shall eventually, like Thomas, come out of that uncomfortable situation to exclaim, "My Lord and my God."

As I testified about the wisdom of God, then came these words: sharma, kuriana, mahinda, kurima and yanda. They came out of my mouth as the tongue or language of the Spirit of God. Then, I wrote them as I heard. Having Googled these strange words and found their meaning, I observed they matched what I was communicating. Sharma—this could mean bliss, happiness, warmth; kuriana—I checked this out to see if I could find the meaning and I saw that it was derived from the Greek word *Kyriakos,* which means "of the Lord" with reference to Jesus Christ, also meaning new experiences, versatile, and generous; Mahinda—this means conqueror of the world, having great power, possessing might; kurima means to till, to plough, a person with huge energy, chestnut, virility and beauty, truth, reality, genuine, without lies, innovation, courage.

I found out that yanda in the Xhosa language of South Africa means expansion, growth, prosperity, multiplication, while in the Philippines, yanda means progress. Also, I found out that the word yanda entails the desire not just for personal success but for leaving a mark in the world. In Hebrew, it is spelt *yada* or Greek *ginosko*—"to know by experience." Bibletools. org, quoting from Daniel 11:32, stated that yanda in the Bible "indicates a combination of close, warm, and even passionate intimacy, combined with head knowledge that produces an edge in a person's life that enables him to trust God and at the same time perceive what He is doing." Yanda also means rock, cliff, God's grace. It stands for idealism, intuition, generosity, creativity, wisdom, and tolerance.

These were the words that the Spirit of God spoke to me as I was inspired to encourage people in this chapter of my book.

The words sharma, kuriana, mahinda, kurima, and yanda, as have been interpreted here, signify God's anointing and blessings that would be upon those who would read, believe, and assimilate this book. Indeed, to my amazement, I never heard these strange words prior to the time of writing this chapter of the book. Situations like this could be why part of the lyrics of a gospel song in my native language, Igbo, states, "Egwu Chukwu na atum," indicating that the singer is afraid of God. I also got afraid of God as I looked up the meaning of each strange word or language that I wrote as mentioned by the Spirit of God.

This is simply God's divine stamp affirming the relevance of this book, especially regarding the place of wisdom in everyone's life. It is a true example of what was written in the Word of God that the Holy Spirit helps us to groan, "Abba! Father," and communicate what is in our minds to God. Equally, what is in the mind of God is revealed to us by His Spirit.

Dear fellow pilgrim, therefore, make good use of this opportunity and assimilate all that has been written in this book. I must say, I see it as a rare opportunity.

When Paul encountered the power of God, he said what he desired was to know Jesus and the power of His resurrection. The experience is so exhilarating. Simon Peter concurred when he said: "Master, to whom shall we go? You have the words of eternal life." Also, in Luke 9:33 (NABRE), he said: "Master, it is good that we are here; and let's make three tabernacles: one for You, one for Moses, and one for Elijah." Peter's experience could be likened to the beauty and splendor of receiving new life in the Spirit, new experiences (Kurian).

Mary the mother of Jesus and Mother of the World was so full of grace and would advise that all mankind should always do the will of God. She was a good example when the angel Gabriel greeted her and passed the message sent from God to her, that she shall conceive by the power of the Holy Spirit to bear a son and shall name Him Jesus. "He will be great and will be called Son of the Most High, the Lord God will give Him the throne of David His father, He will rule over the house of Jacob forever, and of His Kingdom there will be no end." After interacting with the angel, Blessed Mother Mary agreed by saying, "Behold, I am the Handmaid of the Lord. May it be done according to your word." Luke 1:38 (NABRE).

As the Catholic prayer goes, "O Mary conceived without sin, pray for us who have recourse to you." Indeed, my love for her is beyond what words can express. She has been firm in giving me instructions on the pathway to Christ's Sacred Heart. She does not compromise standards yet her expression of love and inexhaustible heart to receive everyone endeared me to her right from age seven—my Block Rosary days till this date.

I have never been ashamed or restrained to tell how sweet and splendid she is when you allow her a place in your life. You may honor her as the mother of Christ and as that mother who knows how to intercede successfully on your behalf to God and His Christ. She fully understands the operations of the Holy Spirit in such a way that when you adopt her meek and humble nature, you will be in the best relationship with the Holy Spirit. By praying and sharing testimonies of her sweet nature many times, people request that I offer more of these prayers/teachings with them because of the great effects in their lives. This proves that even God appreciates the honor being given to the Blessed Mother Mary. May God continue to be praised for creating a woman/mother as herself, so unique and unrivalled, the one whose offspring bruised the head of the old serpent.

The Significance of the Story of the Israelites' Journey to the Promised Land (Canaan) as It Relates to a Pilgrim's Journey

In Numbers Chapter 14 verses 6–9, twelve spies went to spy the land of Canaan. Ten out of twelve reported that they were like grasshoppers before the people living in Canaan because they were giants. However, Joshua and Caleb exclaimed that the land can be conquered; though they did not refute the claim of the other ten spies who reported seeing giants who were descendants of Anak. Joshua said: "If the Lord is pleased with us, then He will bring us into this land and give it to us—a land which flows with milk and honey. Only do not rebel against the Lord; and do not fear the people of the land, for they will be our prey. Their protection is gone from them, and the Lord is with us; do not fear them." Numbers 14:8–9 (NABRE).

The lessons:

1. First, God must be with us.

2. We must believe in what He can do, and He will do it.

3. When God is to destroy giants both spiritual and physical, He removes their power. Giants become ants. The case of David and Goliath is an example.

4. Caleb and Joshua understood these facts and since God was with them, they were turned to multitude of giants and the so-called giants indeed turned to mere ants.

In the journey of a pilgrim and when conquering new grounds, it does not matter what seemed to be there. The concern should rather be having the favor of God, the Yahweh Sabaoth, the Baal Perazim, the Elohim, the ark of the covenant. If God is with us, the giants on our pilgrim journey shall turn little. Just as Goliath became little before David as he moved against him with the power of God; Pharaoh was overpowered at Moses's presence; the chains on Peter in the prison gave way by God's power. The heated furnace became cool for Shadrach, Meshach, and Abednego when they were thrown into the fire.

It is my prayer that every giant—spiritual or physical—existing on our promised land shall turn to an ant. Therefore, move and occupy without fear because the Triumphant King of Ages is with us. Any presumable giant existing in our promised land, at work or home, in our destiny, Christian journey, business, academic pursuit, visions, and aspirations, let them melt like wax before fire. Victory is for all who believe, and this victory is sure.

Pause and Reflect

Life's journey is filled with moments where God's presence is undeniable. Whether through personal testimonies, symbolic revelations, or divine wisdom, He constantly reminds us of His faithfulness. In this chapter, you've encountered stories that illuminate God's ability to guide, provide, and reveal Himself in extraordinary ways. Now, take a moment to pause and reflect on your own journey. How has God spoken to you? What signs has He placed along your path?

Reflection Questions:

1. Can you recall a personal testimony where God's hand was evident in your life? How did that experience strengthen your faith?

2. Have you ever experienced a symbolic moment, dream, or sign that you believed was from God? What message did you receive from it?

3. How has wisdom—whether from scripture, life lessons, or spiritual mentors—helped shape your faith journey?

4. What obstacles or doubts have kept you from fully embracing God's divine guidance in your life?

5. What steps can you take to be more receptive to God's presence and revelations in your daily walk?

Chapter 8

BLESSED MOTHER MARY: "WHITE LILY"

"Mary said, 'Behold, I am the handmaid of the Lord. May it be done to me according to your word." Luke 1:38 (NABRE)

I have included in this book some of the messages and lessons the Holy Spirit taught me. These life-changing messages have truly assisted me in no small way in navigating as a pilgrim.

They have been used to inspire some others on various occasions in my capacity as an evangelizer and prayer intercessor to the glory of God. Most of these people confessed that they were effectively inspired and highly rejuvenated.

To this end, I decided to reach out to more people by including some of my inspired teachings and revelations in this book. It is my belief that you too will be inspired in no small measure.

The Grace Derived as Christian Pilgrims When We Implore the Intercession of Blessed Mother Mary (The Precious White Lily)

Why did I call Blessed Mother Mary the Precious White Lily?

One night, when I was ready to have my night prayers in order to retire for the day, just as I made the sign of the cross in the name of the Father, Son, and Holy Spirit, I heard these gentle but firm words: "White Lily." I continued with my prayers and slept for the night. In the wake of the day, my mind could not escape those words, "White Lily." This continued through my activities of the day, and I decided to check on what these words really were. I found out that the white lily, known as *"Lilium candidum"* or "Madonna lily," is a very beautiful flowering plant native to the Mediterranean, Middle East, and Asia. The flower is used as medicine for back pain, bleeding, and healing of wounds.

It represents purity, innocence, and rebirth. In religious belief, the white lily represents the Virgin Mary and depicts the Resurrection of Christ. It also represents femininity and fertility.

Amongst all the significance given to the white lily, what caught my attention was its status as a symbol of the Blessed Mother Mary. It then made great sense why I heard "white lily" as I did the sign of the cross. So, I wanted to know more why she was called White Lily, which I believe would enable me to understand the message those words were communicating to me directly.

On further study, I found that there was a revelation from St. Gertrude the Great, as an excerpt from the Revelations of St. Gertrude, Book 3, Chapter 18 had revealed. It was during prayer she saw our Blessed Mother in the form of a white lily with three branches, one standing erect, and the other two bent down. This revelation of St Gertrude the Great brought about this title "the Immaculate Lily of the Most Holy Trinity." The saint learned on that occasion that the blinding whiteness of the lily signified the immaculate purity of the Holy Mother of God which was never stained with even the slightest venial sin. The upright leaf of the lily represented the omnipotence of God the Father, and the two leaves which bent down, the wisdom of the Son and the charity of the Holy Spirit. Then Our Blessed Mother spoke to St. Gertrude and said:

"To any soul who faithfully prays the three Hail Marys, I will appear at the hour of death in a splendor so extraordinary that it will fill the soul with heavenly consolation."

From that time, Saint Gertrude saluted the Holy Virgin or her images with the words below:

"Hail White Lily of the ever peaceful and glorious Trinity! Hail, effulgent rose, the delight of Heaven, of whom the King of Heaven was born and by whose milk He was nourished! Nourish our souls by the effusions of thy Divine influences."

The three Hail Marys are said followed by "O my Mother, preserve me from mortal sin during the day." This is prayed in the morning. In the evening, three Hail Marys are prayed along with: "O my Mother, preserve me from mortal sin during this night." This prayer honors the Trinity (God the Father, the Son, and the Holy Spirit).

Having researched and understood this, it gave me the assurance that the voice I heard which said "White Lily" while I was praying was never vain. **I was being informed that the presence of the Trinity One God was with me in union with our Blessed Mother Mary.** How fortunate I am to be carried into their presence. I humbly adore, Oh White Lily of the Holy Trinity.

Due to this revelation, I had to purchase some lily flowers and place them in my room. Even now, I hope to know more about this mystery being revealed to me.

When you implore the Blessed Mother Mary's intercession, the grace to achieve what you most desire even in very difficult circumstances will be possible.

The angel Gabriel in his salutation to her said, "Hail, full of grace . . ." She, of her own account, said: "From now on, ALL generations shall call me blessed." She manifested these attributes especially at the wedding in Cana in John Chapter 2. Though it was not time for Christ to begin His work on earth (meaning the divine appointed time was yet to come), because she was full of grace, she understood that nothing was impossible for her to achieve whenever she requested anything from Her son. For instance, she said: "Son, they had no wine." Then, she went to the servants at the wedding and said: "Do whatever He asks you to do."

First, Christ did as she requested because the Blessed Mother Mary who was already full of grace had the "grace of God within her" activated immediately. This happened as it should, hence, the best wine ever produced became available by Christ turning water to wine. This marked His first miracle. There is a local parlance that says: "Follow the person that knows the way." Indeed, our Blessed Mother Mary knows the way. When you recognize this great secret about her and make good use of it, surely, you will never regret what you did. I am a living witness to her graciousness.

So many wonderful and miraculous things can be attributed to her and so many have already been recorded about her. However, in honor of this great, humble, graceful, principled, compassionate evangelist and mother, I have decided to include one of my teachings about her, which I titled "Virgin Most Prudent."

The Blessed Mother Mary as Virgin Most Prudent has two key words: "most" and "prudent." Most is greatest in amount, while prudent is being wise, discreet, sober, circumspect.

When it is said that someone is prudent, it indicates that the person could judge between virtuous and vicious actions, not only in a general sense but as it regards specific actions at a given time and place.

Blessed Mother Mary's title as Virgin Most Prudent means a virgin or maiden who has the greatest value/virtue in wisdom, discipline, sincerity, justice, obedience, care, integrity, and accountability. This title was deliberately chosen for her by the Church and was very true in every sense of the word considering her history as a maiden while physically on earth; as a mother of the Savior; as a believer of God and as a triumphant saint who was assumed body and soul into heaven.

With that said, let's briefly see some specific actions of the Blessed Mother Mary in the Bible that meritoriously earned her the title Virgin Most Prudent.

Virgin Most Prudent Because She Made the Best and Wisest Eternal Decision (Luke Chapter 1 Verse 26 to 38): What transpired between the angel Gabriel and the Virgin Mary was quite complex and a very difficult request. Despite the danger posed on her literally by accepting that request (considering that she was an unmarried virgin, though already betrothed to Joseph), she was able to look past the danger which could have led to her being stoned to death and accepted God's will. She said in verse 38, "Behold, I am the Handmaid of the Lord. May it be done to me according to your word." Up till today and to eternity, her decision was considered prudent. It was a bold and wise decision. It was a decision of someone who was totally dedicated to God. It was a decision of selflessness, unconditional love, service to God and all human races. It was a decision of total obedience and humility. It was a just decision because she thought of the future prudently. It was a decision of one who was preached to and one who showed she fully understood God's mission for her. For this, the Bible said she bore everything in her heart (Luke 2 verse 19). She became the second Eve, whose son bruised the head of the serpent. Alleluia!

Virgin Most Prudent Because She Is an Ardent Evangelizer for God's Kingdom: She does her ardent evangelical mission with relentless compassion. If I should judiciously throw light about this, a few lines here would not be enough, but I will try a little and hope my points will be understood and used to relate with your own personal experiences. Meditating on John Chapter 2 verse 5, "Do whatever He asks you to do," you will notice the pattern of Blessed Mother Mary's level of prudence.

First, at the wedding, she came just as anyone else—a guest. When she noticed that the wine to serve guests for the occasion had finished (not that she was specifically approached) her compassionate and maternal instinct played out immediately. She was filled with empathy as to the level of disgrace that was about to befall the couple. She immediately got involved to avert the looming shame. Sure, when you invite her into all your matters, even when you are unaware of impending danger, she steps in and averts such danger expeditiously.

Secondly, she knew when and how to get something from God. Remember, she is prudent (wise and judicious). One who is prudent always see beyond the ordinary. Though it was not Christ's time, He performed the miracle; it was not only because she asked or because she was the mother of Christ, but she came from the place of unconditional love, had clear discernment of the whole situation, and saw the answer to that precarious moment long before anyone else could (having insight and foresight). Through this, she made her son, who was still waiting for His time, commence his mission work immediately. Assessing by this action, she assisted in shaping the active commencement of Christ's mission. It was a situation of, "Why shift for tomorrow what you can do today?" When you have recourse to her, she will shape your thoughts and guide you through a fulfilling pilgrim mission.

Remember, despite Christ's response to her, she still went ahead and said to the servants at the wedding, "Do whatever (don't doubt, just do it) He asks you to do." How did she know that Jesus would grant her request? How did she know that the process of actualizing the miracle would not be the usual way? These questions are deep but have already been answered above, if you had read discerningly. However, let me say it again: the answer is that she is Most Prudent, and this grants her access to hidden divine secrets and understanding of deep mysteries. Of course, she is called the Mystical Rose (Rosa Mystica). The White Lily whose heart is always connected to the Trinity. She simply sees what others do not see. Glory! When you let her into your space unrestricted—not despised, as some do due to lack of understanding about who she truly is—she will teach you hidden divine wisdom and how to apply it for both your earthly and heavenly bliss. Invite her today and end the ignorance.

In all my knowledge about her, she NEVER spoke about herself. She would direct you to God and her son Jesus Christ. Just as I wrote earlier. First, she went to her son. Then, she referred the servants to her son, asking them to obey His words. You may ask yourself, given the first response she received from Christ, why did she still go ahead to tell the servants at the wedding to do whatever Christ asked them to do? That was a serious walk of faith. How did she know that Christ would honor her request? Not only that, but she also revealed to them the secret to get the miracle done—"Do whatever He asks you to do." Glory! Up until today, in all her apparitions, even when she spoke to the visioners, never did she talk about herself. She always would come with messages, reminding humanity to follow the footsteps of Christ. She would encourage everyone to repent. She says to do good in accordance with God's Word. She is indeed selfless, ardent, and an extraordinary evangelizer.

It is quite necessary that all mankind learn from her. If you earnestly observe her true nature and apply her style, surely, you will be at peace with God and achieve whatever is needed for your well-being.

Let me share one of my personal encounters with this ardent evangelizer, compassionate winner of souls for God and His Christ, the Blessed Immaculate, White Lily, Mother Mary, Mother of Christ-the-King.

My personal experiences of her maternal care are, for me, testimonies. Truly, she was the very first person to clearly direct me to follow her son as I have already mentioned in some of the chapters of this book.

Indeed, there is something about this Holy Divine Being called Blessed Mother Mary. It can be seen in her approach to doing things. It is so admirable. When she uses her approach, you will never be able to resist her maternal influence. She is mild, yet firm in her drive. Yes, when she approached me the second time and said those words, I felt entangled. Remember, I mentioned earlier that I made a request that happened exactly as I had desired. My situation could be compared to a man who asked God for twin children—male and female—for a particular month of the year, and behold, there came the twins, the same month and year, male and female. What a shocking and miraculous surprise that would be! This was what happened in my case, however, this time, it was about a school examination. I was overwhelmed and had no excuse logical enough not to obey her invitation. I did not know that she took cognizance of my request. I made that request not with the most serious composure, but God granted it exactly through Mother Mary's intercession.

This, I believe, happened to show once again that God is miraculous, and He is working totally in tandem with the Blessed Mother Mary in upholding His salvation for mankind. I became one of those souls God gave the opportunity to be part of His salvific work. The most thrilling part is that this occurred with the Blessed Mother Mary being the protagonist. This is my true-life story.

Blessed Mother Mary's sublime softness is worthy of emulation. Take a moment to think about her words during her second visit to me: "You have got what you asked for; I want you to follow my son." This came across to me as mild but very impactful. One can understand better how this kind of approach melted Jesus's heart at the wedding in Cana of Galilee. She understands that the secret of God's kingdom is righteousness, peace and joy in the Holy Ghost, and she makes maximum use of the tenets.

Blessed Mother Mary follows through when she steps into a matter, just as she did at the wedding in Cana. She took my request to her son, who granted it expressly. The Blessed Mother Mary was so committed to see that I was converted totally to God. Was she successful? Yes, she was successful. She achieved her purpose, as is always the case.

The secret is, get to know what is expected of you and do it—then your peace is assured. Do you know what happens when there is tranquility within you? Undaunted success will follow you. Frankly, I did not only follow her son; I got groomed to also become an evangelizer of the good news of Christ, a prayer warrior, and one under a great mission for conversion of souls for God's kingdom through teaching what I have learnt by the power of the Holy Spirit. Part of the evidence are these solemn thoughts that I have shared with you here in book form. I invite you to follow Christ the Savior of the world. You will never regret answering the call to follow Christ the King.

So, you now understand why one will say, "Hail Mary full of grace, the Lord is with you, blessed are you among women and blessed is the fruit of your womb Jesus, Holy Mary, Mother of God, pray for us sinners, now and at the hour of death. Amen." It does not mean one cannot go directly to Christ and God Almighty. One can and should, really. However, when it looks like it may not be easy to go directly to Jesus or God, you should implore her maternal help to intercede on your behalf to God and through her son Jesus Christ. I assure you, once she steps in, consider that matter settled. If, while on earth, the Bible recorded that she intervened in a lack of wine at the wedding in Cana of Galilee and there was an immediate solution that yielded the best results, you can imagine the benefit one stands to get now that she is in heaven in her total divine state. That we go to our earthly mothers most often so that they plead before our earthly father for a request to be granted does not mean we cannot ask our dad directly. Sometimes, we feel Mum can get it faster, especially when we feel Dad may not want to give it to us immediately.

Virgin Most Prudent Because She Is the Ideal Divine Mirror and Model for Humanity: Blessed Virgin Mary is not only the most prudent but the most invaluable of God's creatures. Her offspring bruised the head of the serpent and helped humanity to regain a cordial relationship with God. Her relentless pursuit of souls for God's kingdom has appeared in many places all over the world with one distinct message: follow my son Jesus Christ. Her emphasis is on loving and obeying the commandments of God. While on earth, she obeyed these commandments of God through various exemplary actions written of her in the Bible. She, to this day, talks to human beings (of which I am a witness) in our minds, through dreams, visions, physical apparitions. For example, it was written that at Fatima in 1917, she appeared to three children—Lucia, Jacinta, and Francis—with a message requesting them to constantly pray and do penance for the sins of the world and conversion of souls. She also said they should always pray for peace in the world. In 1992, she appeared in Nigeria at Aokpe (a place in Benue State) to a visionary, Christiana Agbo, with the same message of the need for repentance of sinners. The most significant of the miracles were the movement of the sun and healing from holy spring water at the site of her appearance. Similar miracles and appearances have been recorded at Lourdes in France, Guadalupe, and so many other places.

She has appeared physically to individuals as well. My dad, Sir Eugene Augustine Onyeachufulenwanneya Obiegbu Ksj of blessed memory, once told me how our Blessed Mother Mary appeared to him physically. This happened according to him when he was in the place of prayer, in his forties, and was the president of the Legion of Mary. He recounted being so frightened that he ran away and did not return to his room until three days had passed. The Blessed Mother Mary is indeed real and undoubtedly appears to those she chose to show her divine presence. I have also seen her in my dream where she handed me two green mangoes and I knelt to receive them. As she was going, I immediately recovered from the ecstasy, ran after her, and said, "Mother bless me." She looked at me and blessed me with the sign of the cross (signifying "I bless you in the name of the Father, Son, and Holy Spirit"). It is pertinent to note here that she did not bless me when I requested, using her own name or anything contrary. Rather, she invoked the Trinitarian God (God the Father, God the Son, and God the Holy Spirit) by making the sign of the cross. Glory!

Being prudent comprises all other good virtues, be it love, faith, hope, etcetera. When one is prudent, you will think before you talk. Issues are properly weighed, and best options taken within the confines of the law or what is appropriate. Right decisions elicit right actions.

It is most ideal for everyone to mirror the Blessed Mother Mary as the ideal model or divine mirror in life, especially as it relates to the relationship with God and humanity. Her maternal role in the body of Christ cannot be overemphasized. Ask for her help always knowing that we are just pilgrims on earth. I ask her equally for her intercession on your behalf, that God will grant your heart's desires most speedily through Christ the Lord.

In honor of our Blessed Mother Mary, sing this Catholic song:

"Ave Maria, gratia plena, dominus tecum, benedicta tu."

"As I kneel before you, as I bow my head in prayer, take this day, make it yours, and fill me with your love."

Pause and Reflect

Mary, the Blessed Mother, exemplifies humility, obedience, and unwavering faith. She was chosen to bear the Savior of the world, not because of status or wealth, but because of her purity of heart and submission to God's will. Her life is a testament to the power of saying *yes* to God, even when the path is uncertain.

As you reflect on this chapter, consider how Mary's virtues can inspire your own faith journey. Her wisdom and prudence teach us that true strength is found in trust and surrender to God's divine plan.

Reflection Questions:

1. In what ways does Mary's humility and obedience inspire your faith walk?

2. How can you cultivate purity of heart and trust in God's plan, even in uncertain times?

3. Mary pondered things in her heart (Luke 2:19). How do you take time to reflect on God's work in your life?

4. What challenges make it difficult for you to fully surrender to God's will?

5. How can you emulate Mary's role as a vessel of God's grace in your daily interactions with others?

Chapter 9

REFINED IN THE WILDERNESS

"Remember how for these forty years the Lord, your God, has directed all your journeying in the wilderness, so as to test you by affliction, to know what was in your heart: to keep his commandments, or not." Deuteronomy 8:2 (NABRE)

Life brings various phases in the human journey. Sometimes it is rosy, neutral, painful, or joyful. Whatever phase you find, if such phase has been destined, it is for a purpose. Once it has been destined, it cannot be avoided, be it the phase of pain or joy. You cannot choose only joyful moments in the journey of life. In the same way, it cannot always be pain or neutrality. So sometimes this pain period, as a believer of Christ, could be vague. You may not be able to fathom why things went badly even when you try hard to figure it out. You may pray fervently for God to show you what the uncomfortable state is about, but there would be utmost silence from God. When you seek help from those around you, expecting them to shed light on the ugly phase you are going through, unfortunately, they will have no fruitful answer for you.

At a time in my journey as a pilgrim, I found myself in this kind of situation—a wilderness phase of life. There was a senior colleague of mine that was highly gifted with the heart of encouragement. I remembered the low stage I was in at the time, and when I encountered this person, appropriate words were used to lighten my mood. I sometimes wondered what kind of being sees an unfavorable moment and tells you, no, it is not bad at all—rather, all that presented themselves around you were sparkling stars waiting to guide you to your place of abundance. I would try to oppose the opinion, but this person remained resolute that what I considered dryness at that time, or insufficient progress, was practice towards abundant blessings. I wondered then what kind of person would say to laugh or rejoice when you have just lost an opportunity. However, no matter how heavy the burden was then, I always felt very light and strengthened to keep hope alive. The encouragement I received through positive words would come into me as seed and renew me. Hence, when I go into low moments, I remember those encouraging words and desire to hear more. Unfortunately, we lost contact.

A wilderness experience is a very terrible, difficult experience that is traumatic as a believer of Christ on an earthly journey. At one time or another in your life on this journey, you will surely encounter a wilderness experience.

Though I cannot compare exactly the weight of Jesus Christ's pain from the Garden of Gethsemane to Golgotha, imagining a bit of it is necessary to enable you to understand wilderness experiences. This is when it feels like you are all alone. No help comes, and when assistance does come, it makes no sense, because that is not the solution to the challenge you are confronted with. It is a period of total dryness. Even Jesus, despite an angel coming to strengthen Him at the Garden of Gethsemane, once cried on the cross, "Eloi Eloi Lama Sabachthani" ("My God, my God, why have you forsaken me").

Surely, during the period of your wilderness experience, you would feel forsaken and empty. Coincidentally, it is a must-take route should you really want to emerge a strong and victorious Christian pilgrim.

I observed that most often, God tends to keep quiet when one is going through this experience. He does not want to reveal all the challenges you will face on the journey so that there is no unnecessary fear or discouragement regarding the perils on the road. God knows that if you trust Him, you will surely come out victorious from the wilderness stage of life. Jesus saw clearly His own wilderness stage. When He did, he exclaimed, "Oh Father, if it's my will, I would not drink this cup. However not my will but your will be done." Indeed, the Father did His will and today the result is our salvation, which was won for us by Christ agreeing to go through His own wilderness experience. Everyone's wilderness experience is not the same. There are various distinct measures for everyone.

God, in His infinite wisdom, makes wilderness experiences kind of blank. That is why no clear answers are given as to what one will encounter once it is the time for the wilderness experience phase. Consider the experience of the Israelites when God delivered them from slavery in Egypt and they were going to Canaan the Promised Land. There was a shorter way to the promised land, but God said no. He would not let them take the shorter way because there were enemies—the Philistines were on the way. They would oppose and annihilate them, so God allowed them to go through the wilderness because it was a safer route. While going through the wilderness, the Israelites were agonizing. All God was doing for them was not appreciated by most. They did not know that within that period, it was better for them to suffer a bit and live than go presumably faster and all perish.

Consequently, the parting of the Red Sea for them to get through safely did not matter. The miracle of provision of water from rock did not matter. The manna and quail provision did not matter. The pillar of cloud by day and pillar of fire by night did not matter. All the miracles that they witnessed while in that wilderness never were appreciated. They just wanted to leave the wilderness and find themselves in Canaan the Promised Land. They never appreciated that they were being safeguarded from ravenous beasts and dreaded enemies who did not want any of them to survive. For instance, in Exodus 13:17–22 (New American Standard Bible—NASB 1995), it says: "Now when Pharaoh had let the people go, God did not lead them by the way of the land of the Philistines even though it was near; for God said, the people might change their minds when they see war and return to Egypt. Hence God led the people around by the way of the wilderness to the Red Sea..."

In one's wilderness experience, sometimes, you may ask God, why have you abandoned me? Why is it that I cannot perceive or visualize the cause of this challenge or delay? Why is a solution for easy escape or to alleviate the discomforting situation elusive?

Take it that God hid the dangers on the way because if you see them, most likely you would not embark on the journey. The journey, despite the perils, is a must for you to reach your full potential.

A wilderness experience is necessary to fulfil destiny. Equally, it would enable you to accomplish your goal. It helps one to be purified, strong, equipped, and formidable, as expected of a child of God. Once you go through the wilderness experience and come out successful, you become a gallant Christian pilgrim worthy of your call.

It is expected that the golden knowledge I have shared with you in this book will grant you sufficient wisdom to journey successfully. When you do face your wilderness experience, savor every moment, reflect on each moment, take notes, and learn. Whatever you have learnt will assist you in no small way in conquering new grounds. Each lesson will be the golden key required to open doors in other phases of life. Wilderness experience indeed enables one to receive the needed tutelage to live a fulfilled life at a higher level.

This song by Charles Albert Tindley (1905) titled "By and By" just dropped in my spirit:

Refrain: "By and by, when the morning comes, when the saints of God are gathered home, we'll tell the story how we've overcome, for we'll understand it better by and by."

Pause and Reflect

The wilderness is often seen as a place of struggle, uncertainty, and isolation, yet it is also a season of deep spiritual growth and divine preparation. Throughout the Bible, God led His people through the wilderness—not to abandon them, but to refine them, strengthen their faith, and teach them complete reliance on Him.

Your own wilderness season may involve trials, delays, or personal battles that test your endurance and faith. But just as God provided for Israel, comforted Elijah, and prepared Jesus for His ministry, He is also working in your wilderness experience.

Reflection Questions:

1. Have you ever experienced a "wilderness season" in your life? How did it challenge or change you?

2. What lessons do you think God is teaching you through difficult or uncertain times?

3. How do you typically respond when you feel spiritually dry or distant from God?

4. What biblical examples of perseverance in the wilderness inspire you to keep trusting in God's plan?

5. How can you shift your perspective to see your wilderness season as a time of preparation rather than punishment?

Chapter 10

THE FAITHFULNESS OF GOD, THE SOWER'S STORY, AND THE RAPTURE

"Know, then, that the Lord, your God, is God: the faithful God who keeps covenant mercy to the thousandth generation toward those who love him and keep his commandments."
Deuteronomy 7:9 (NABRE)

In the Bible, Hebrews 10:23, it says: "Let us hold fast the confession of our hope without wavering for He who promised is faithful." Equally, in Psalm 33:4, it says: "For the Word of the Lord is upright and His work is done in faithfulness." These two scriptural passages captured key points that I intend to write on briefly.

First, what is faithfulness? Faithfulness is the quality of being steadfast, firm in adherence to promises. It entails reliability, commitment, truth, and allegiance. For the purpose of this message, God is considered here—known and adjudged faithfulness personified. God is our mirror. His faithfulness is seen as you look at the firmament. You see God's faithfulness as you behold the composition of the human being. This faithfulness is seen in the environment, in the climate, as one breathes free air, natural oxygen given to human beings by God. God's faithfulness is seen in the Word of God. Day in and day out, things happen that depict God's faithfulness. So, God is our mirror when one tries to understand what faithfulness represents.

How has God shown that He is faithful?

1. God is a covenant/promise-keeping God. Through the Bible in several chapters, man's encounter with God has proven Him to be faithful. For instance, in Genesis 22:17, God told Abraham that: "I will surely bless you and make your descendants numerous as the stars in the sky and as sand on the seashore." That was one of the promises God made. Did He keep this covenant? Did He keep this promise with Abraham? Yes, God did. The Bible recorded that God fulfilled that promise when He gave Abraham Isaac. Then Isaac begat Esau and Jacob. Esau had his own children, and they kept multiplying. Jacob had twelve children and these twelve children begot more children, and they kept increasing in population. It can be seen today that the people of Israel are so many and everywhere, fulfilling the promise that the descendants of Abraham shall be so uncountable—numerous as stars in the sky and sand on the seashore.

2. God also said to the Israelites that he would give them the land of Canaan. The Promised Land, filled with milk and honey. Did He do it? Yes, He did. In Joshua Chapter

5 verse 13 to Chapter 6 verse 27, God took the Israelites through Jericho into the Promised Land. Even when the people of Jericho stood against them from passing freely through their city and were ready to fight the Israelites just to hinder them from entering the promised land God had assured them of, God Himself arose and sent His own army to pull down the wall of Jericho by His glorious presence and the Israelites passed safely into Canaan. In Joshua Chapter 5:13–14, Joshua saw a man standing and he went to the man and asked, "Are you for us or for our enemies?" In verse 14, the man replied, "I am here as Commander of the Lord's Army." So, the Israelites did not need to fight to enter the promised land. It was God Himself who through His might and miraculous power fought their enemies and gave them free passage. God cannot repent. He does not go back on His promises. To further prove that it was God's power at work, the man asked Joshua to remove his sandal because he was standing on holy ground. The Israelites were told to march around the city of Jericho and on the seventh time, they had to blast the trumpet as God commanded them.

3. Another way God proves His faithfulness is by bringing what is not in existence into existence. God proves His faithfulness in uncommon situations by bringing that which is uncommon to fruition. In Luke Chapter 1 verse 37, the Word of God said "for with God nothing shall be impossible." Luke 1 verses 26 to 33 were about the encounter the Blessed Virgin Mary had with angel Gabriel. There, the angel told her that she would conceive and bear a son who shall be called Emmanuel. He would be the Messiah, Christ, who would save the whole world. The Blessed Virgin Mary then asked, "How could this be when I am a virgin?" Then, the angel replied that she shall be overshadowed by the power of the Holy Spirit. This encounter proved that Christ came in an uncommon way.

Biologically, it was impossible, but with God, all things are possible.

So, God manifests His power and faithfulness by bringing forth things not in existence into existence. By causing uncommon things to come into fruition.

God, in simple terms, calls us always to live the life of faithfulness. He reminds mankind to visualize Him and see His love for human beings, for God so loves the world that He gave His only begotten son that whosoever believes in Him will not perish but have everlasting life. This kind of love expressed by God is an act of faithfulness. To redeem mankind—who has fallen away from God's commandments—to prevent them from going into oblivion or being condemned, and to restore mankind to life, Christ was the only One fit and able to open the scroll in order to rescue the fallen human beings. This is a sign of God's love and faithfulness.

God has never ceased from calling mankind to come out from their unfaithful life. Such a life is filled with rancor, jealousy, gossip, greed, covetousness, insincere feelings towards others, and having old apparel or improper behavior aligned with old ways of doing things. A life that pretends to be genuine when in reality it is a situation of a wolf in sheep's clothing. These features are totally unacceptable to God and He calls mankind today as always to desist and live a faithful, sincere life just as He has demonstrated since the beginning of time. God admonishes everyone to be real both in the open and in secret. Mankind is required to always be truthful. God is very unhappy when human beings turn against each other through a life of unfaithfulness, no matter the reason one may adduce as to why the person would act untruly.

So, the time is now when God calls again for a return to Him unto a life of faithfulness—a request to totally turn away from acts of wrongdoing, immoral behavior, acts that are dishonorable, and anything that devalues the dignity of man.

God expects man to live a life that is pleasing to Him. A life in accordance with His commandments.

The Creator of heaven and earth and all that is in it wants to be proud of mankind, the people He can call His faithful children. Therefore, if anyone desires a life of peace and love, it is expected that the person should live a life that is faithful. This is by being sincere and obeying His commandments. Sincerity, as I mean it here, is loving God and those we encounter as we live here on earth. It is indeed mandatory for Christ's followers to be found trustworthy.

Therefore, it is written in 1 Corinthians 5:7 (NABRE): "Clean out the old yeast, so that you may become a fresh batch of dough, in as much as you are unleavened. For our paschal lamb, Christ, has been sacrificed." God is desirous of faithful servants, those who He would rely on to propagate His kingdom on earth. It is most ideal that one understands the significance of faithfulness and imbibe it for successful living.

My Understanding of the Parable of the Sower:

I want to share some extra knowledge I got from the Holy Spirit about the parable of the sower in Matthew 13:1–23.

After reading this passage, I formed some questions, such as:

1. Who is a Pharisee?

2. Since the sower was the one planting, why did the sower allow some seeds to fall on the pathway, some on rock, some on thorns, some on good soil?

3. Why didn't the sower just put all the seeds on good soil?

4. Are the other seeds that fell elsewhere supposed to be blamed?

I really needed answers, especially regarding the seeds. So, I relaxed to hear, and boom—it was as if the Holy Spirit said to me, "You should know the answers to these questions." Then, in a flash (as is typical with wisdom), the answers were provided.

Firstly, the Pharisees are those who know the laws/words of God and pride themselves in it. They have several years of experience in handling things of God. They have a history of how they were told God operated with His people, yet Jesus referred to them as those who look but could not see. They heard but learnt nothing. They were regarded as being complacent with things of God. So, Christ spoke to them in parables to get them more confused. He felt they had so much learning yet did not know how to make good use of the knowledge acquired. Here, the question "who is a Pharisee" connotes therefore that a Pharisee would be someone whom God has taught so many mysteries. The person whom God expects to have a good understanding of His laws and practice them completely in such a way that pleases Him. The person who has shown little or no proper stewardship.

The second question I asked was if the sower was planting, why did the sower allow some seeds to fall on pathway, some on rock, some on thorns, some on good soil? The answer I got for this second question guided me in the other adjoining questions.

The Holy Spirit told me immediately, without waiting for me to finish my thought. He said that:

1. All seeds the sower had initially were very good. None of the seeds were bad.

2. All the seeds were planted with good intentions. They had no reason not to turn good or fall on good soil to bear good fruits, because they were good seeds.

3. The sower sowed them as good seeds but the choice of position and what happened to them after was not the sower's decision. The duty of the sower was to provide good seed. The seeds were planted. While some turned out very well, some seeds came out bad or unproductive because they took wrong positions out of a choice different from that of the sower.

4. Those seeds that fell elsewhere had misdirected destiny caused by their own greed, selfishness, and lackadaisical attitude. They forgot what they were and made the sower very sad. Not only that they did not bear fruits, but they also died on the way without fulfilling their purpose— that is, without being productive.

5. The seeds that fell on the pathway were eaten by birds of the air. These birds are seen as ravenous beasts, destiny destroyers, satanic agents. These agents noticed that they had no divine protection anymore.

The question again is what actions did humanity take that made some lose divine protection? Their action or inaction may have resulted in them being vulnerable to ravenous beasts. This was the case of the seed that fell on the pathway which was eaten by birds of the air. May God have mercy! These enemies when they find out that you lack divine protection due to wrong choices made or due to loss of focus, surely, they do not spare their prey but eat them up. May God help!

How about the seeds that fell on thorns that were choked by the weeds or those on rock that were scourged by the sun, and they died? They fell victim to their worries and ill-advised activities. They are those who prefer to say: "If you can't beat them, join them." These categories of persons need to turn their worries sincerely to God. Do not be afraid to be vulnerable before your Christ; He knows, and He is able to help. He alone deserves to see your tears and concerns. He is too faithful to fail us. Do not show your weaknesses to the world, otherwise, like evil weeds, they would choke you.

God's grace is sufficient for everyone. Turn your weaknesses to God. Seeing your sincerity of heart, He will help. He helped all those before us, so surely, He will intervene now. Mind you, God is still the same yesterday, today, and forever. The I Am.

You really have no excuse to say "God, why didn't you do it this way or that way?" He has given us all. He has shown us the way through His Word. He has created us as good seeds, in His likeness, and saw that we were good. Through His Holy Spirit, God has taught us and reminded us of the ways of our Creator. He asks today, having done all this and more, what is the issue? Why are we not being productive or fruitful as expected of seeds that were originally good? Do not read this question and move on. You are required to take a deep breath, pulse, and answer the question most sincerely. You really have no good reason not to bear fruits, especially now that it is even less risky to mention Jesus's name or preach about the kingdom of God, unlike many centuries back. The disciples, elders, and prophets of God never had this leisure that we have now. They were forbidden to speak or minister in the name of Jesus Christ during their time. So many were annihilated for that reason. Grab the opportunity while the time is still available. There is no excuse.

I asked why the sower did not put all the seeds on the good soil. The right question to ask is, why didn't all the seeds bear fruits in their numbers (since all were initially good)? Why did some seeds fall on the pathway, thorns, and rock, while from the same good seeds came those that fell on good soil and were fruitful? From the numerous and extensive answers already given here, simply, it was clear that the seeds that refused to germinate or do well did so out of a choice contrary to the sower's good intentions.

One is expected to bear good fruits through the kind of life one lives on a daily basis. Life is a gift from God and everyone is responsible for the choices they make by themselves. Therefore, endeavor to make good use of your spiritual gifts, talents, and opportunities, because there is a day of reckoning. A day to give account to the Creator.

A yoke represents the activities of this world that have been put on God's children to derail them and truncate their destinies—may it be destroyed by God's holy fire. May we realize that we were created as good seeds and deserve to bear good fruits in abundance by being kind, by spreading love and the peace of Christ every day. Let us showcase good images in secret and the open. Know that God is watching everyone. He is coming with His recompense. Let's continue to fellowship together most genuinely. Do not fail to tell it all to God. Though He knows all we are doing, He is happy when we express that we believe in Him. Tell it all, show it all to Jesus because if we don't, a time will come when there will not be any hiding place nor excuse granted.

May we not be found wanting and may we not lose our focus here on earth through Christ our Lord who is King forever and ever. Amen.

The Secret of Rapture

On January 25th, 2025, I heard these words in the spirit: "Glory of God." As I listened further, I heard, "It is the glory of God that will help to connect people to the rapture call. Glory of God is the mark that can attract the connection to transform the physical body into another body to meet Christ in the cloud."

Then, I asked, "So who will be raptured?" The answer I got from the Holy Spirit was, "God has no preference regarding whom to rapture; rather, ALL who have the glory of God with them when the trumpet sounds would be connected and raptured (taken into glory)." The Holy Spirit explained rapture to mean "taken into glory."

The important thing to note here is that God has no favorites, and one of the criteria that would enable someone to be raptured—I must say indeed, the most paramount—is to have the mark of God's glory.

What is the Rapture? The Rapture as defined by the Holy Spirit is to be taken into glory. It signifies the second coming of Christ. The Scripture in Matthew 24:30 spoke of the son of Man appearing in the sky with power and great glory. In Titus Chapter 2 verse 13, regarding the second coming of Christ which all believers in Christ await, also known as the Rapture, it states: "looking for the blessed hope and the appearing of the glory of our great God and Savior Jesus Christ." Further scripture reading on this can be seen in 1 Thessalonians Chapter 4 verses 16–17. It states: "The Lord Himself will descend from heaven with a cry of command, with the voice of an archangel, and with the sound of the trumpet of God. And the dead in Christ will rise first. Then we who are alive, who are left, will be caught up together with them in the clouds to meet the Lord in the air, and so we will always be with the Lord."

Taken from the accounts of Matthew chapter 24 verse 30 and Titus Chapter 2 verse 13, which indicated that Christ will appear in power and great glory, this significantly explains why the Holy Spirit revealed that one who is raptured is "taken into glory," and it will be only those covered in God's glory that will be connected to Christ. This is a hidden secret, revealed to me, that I have shared with you. So, get to know what the glory of God is and ensure you always stay in His glory in readiness for that great day of the manifestation of the Son of Man.

What is God's glory? It is the presence of God. His Shekinah. In Hebrew it is called "Kavod"—the power and majesty of God's presence. In Igbo it is called "Ebubechukwu," which means God's glory, while in Greek it is called "Doxa," meaning the radiance or splendor of God.

God's glory is so precious to Him and this can be seen in Isaiah Chapter 42 verse 8 (NABRE) "I am the Lord, Lord is my name; my glory I give to no other, nor my praise to idols." The glory of God signifies God's splendor. It is the symbol of the essence of God. It shows His power, authority, and beauty. It is the mark of God's presence. It distinguishes a believer in Christ from an unbeliever.

Having known this, if anyone lacks the appearance of God's glory, it means the person has lost divine coverage or eligibility to be counted among the heirs of God's kingdom. Moreso, such a person cannot be raptured. To avoid this, seek and remain in God's glory.

Pause and Reflect

God's faithfulness is unwavering, His promises are unchanging, and His word is true. Through the parable of the sower, Jesus teaches us about the condition of our hearts in receiving His truth, and through the mystery of the rapture, we are reminded of the importance of remaining steadfast in our faith.

As you reflect on this chapter, consider how God has shown His faithfulness in your life and how you can ensure that your heart remains fertile ground for His word.

Reflection Questions:

1. How have you personally experienced God's faithfulness in your life?

2. The parable of the sower describes different types of soil. Which best represents the current state of your heart in receiving God's word?

3. How can you cultivate a deeper and more consistent faith in God's promises?

4. What does the concept of the rapture teach you about spiritual readiness?

5. In what ways can you encourage others to trust in God's faithfulness and prepare for His coming?

Chapter u

AND GOD MANIFESTED HIS PRESENCE

"The Lord answered: 'I myself will go along, to give you rest.'" Exodus 33:14 (NABRE)

The crux of this book is to reveal some hidden treasures, lessons to be learnt as one journeys to fulfill the call of destiny while on earth and to imprint the reality that there is an afterlife. What you make out of your journey now determines what you will reap in the future. This phase is enthralling. There are joyous and challenging moments. However, the joy in taking a committed Christian journey far outweighs the challenges. I have tried in this book to assist everyone to understand that these challenges are critical for pruning.

I have shared some of my personal life experiences. I really have felt both sides of the divide. The painful sides have broken me, brought me down, but could not keep me down. Notwithstanding, I do affirm that of all these low moments which were excruciating, when I felt God chose to be silent,

God was not quiet—rather He was restructuring events in my favor.

I indicated in Chapter 6 of this book that at some of those low moments when I felt dried and lonely, on a desert road all by myself with no satisfying comfort, I wallowed as broken internal pieces, my inner thoughts, and my private tears were my constant companions. During these troubling moments in my life, despite my actual circumstance, I looked strong externally. The irony of this situation was when I tried to reveal to some of the people I felt were experienced in such matters, they treated these challenges with levity. They wanted me to hear their own problems than listen to mine. This hurts more than the challenge. Despite the situation, one thing I clearly noticed was that my inner spirit never gave up on me. Just like Psalm 42 verse 11 puts it: "Why are you in despair, my soul? And why are you restless within me? Wait for God, for I will again praise Him . . ." This made me more convinced that the Holy Spirit is indeed man's greatest and faithful companion. The Holy Spirit never departs from any soul. If you listen, even when you sin, the Spirit of God is there to call you back. The Spirit of God gives you unlimited reasons to be convinced as to why you should return or remain on your God-given journey. Especially when you feel you've tried your best, but it seems not to be working as planned and you want to give up.

The signs of giving up start showing when you no longer pray as you should. Also, when you start avoiding the assembly of God's children; not wanting to listen to the Word of God; querying almost everything, even irrelevant things. The thumbs down may be countless, but behold, for me, the Holy Spirit said: "I will not give up on you. You just must be calm and listen. This phase MUST pass, and you will emerge victorious." In my case, in the face of things looking so impossible, I was reminded that if I just hung in there, I would overcome and be restored.

I indicated in one of the chapters of this book how God showed me His strength in my weakest moments by putting various songs in my inner mind, and I often woke up singing them. When I checked the lyrics and meditated on them, the words would come out to be God addressing the specific situation I was facing at that time.

For instance, during one of the weary days, I heard this song: "His Eyes Are On the Sparrows . . ." Yes, indeed God watches over me! So, He watches over you! After hearing this song in my spirit and checking the lyrics, it appeared to be God talking directly to me. As I meditated on the song, some awaited miracles happened a few days later that lightened my heart.

I was also encouraged at a certain time when I had a very clear dream of holy angels and holy ancient saints appearing in twos. They were so close between the sky and earth that in excitement I jumped and wanted to touch them. This happened between the hours of 3:14 a.m. to 5:30 a.m. The holy angels had what looked like a long stick or rod and one of the ancient holy saints was giving out a flower with bold green leaves attached to the stem, freely, to the crowd. I remembered requesting a flower and I made my son get one. My excitement knew no bounds, such that I screamed and said: "See the angels. Are you not seeing them? See the angels! Look at the saints! Ooooh!" I was trying to call the attention of those with me, who seemed not to have seen what I saw. I made a great effort to make them look and be part of my excitement. I mentioned some of the names of the saints. I said: "Oh, look at St. Francis. Oh, see Saint Theresa," and so on. The angels and saints I saw were many. The episode was for me a glorious encounter, an awesome sight to behold. In the wake of the day, I pondered what that encounter was about, and I informed some Christian brethren who thanked God on my behalf for granting me such a rare privilege. Some said they would love to have such an experience in their lifetime.

This goes to show that God is real. The heavenly beings are real too. It also goes to affirm that these beings are with us both when we are aware and not aware. It was evident that I was not alone, and surely no one that believed in God would be abandoned, even in very difficult times.

When everyone seems to have deserted you and you feel all those terrible thoughts running through your mind and almost consuming you, just hang in there. You are never alone. God has got you. Christ has got you. The Holy Spirit has got you. The angels and holy saints of God have got you. Behold the universe of God and all within, which includes but is not limited to the sky, the wind, the sand, the birds—sparrows, hummingbirds, red cardinal birds, falcons, blue birds—squirrels, and the double rainbow (these things brought me positive signs during my very low moment/awaiting period; I testify to this with the utmost sense of responsibility). For instance, I noticed the pattern of the birds. Once they consistently appear around my house or visit my bedroom window, that simply alerts me that something is imminent, and I ask God for good news. Then, not long after, the good news comes. God is indeed great, and I am a living witness.

I am convinced that this book will in no small way revive a weary heart and return you to God no matter how you have drifted in your own journey. The inspiring testimonies I have included in this book will help. Also, Chapter 12 is about words of wisdom from my dad, Chapter 13 is about life and the Ziglar Assessment, and the last chapter centers on some areas of prayer vital to life journey as a pilgrim.

The Pilgrim's Journey is a compendium of divine organic life lessons, experiences, and revelations.

The Exciting Experience During My Pilgrimage in Israel

I had a first-hand encounter while in Israel on pilgrimage in 2009. This got me so convinced that the Bible is not a story of fiction. The stories and encounters as written in the Bible are true.

I traveled on pilgrimage to Israel with about thirty-nine other pilgrims—young and elderly. We had a three-day stay in Jerusalem before moving to Tiberias and we were able to visit various holy sites both in Jerusalem and its surrounding cities. We visited sites such as the birthplace of Jesus Christ in Bethlehem; River Jordan where John baptized Christ; the Wailing Wall (the remaining wall left of Solomon's temple as the contingent narrator explained); we had the opportunity to see the Dome on the Rock, where it was said Abraham tried to sacrifice Isaac as instructed by God but eventually God provided a lamb for the sacrifice instead. We visited the place where Peter's mother in-law had hands laid upon her, and she became healed of her fever. We had the privilege of visiting Elizabeth, Zacharia and John's home. I equally saw the supposed sycamore tree Zacchaeus climbed to see Jesus and Jesus asked him to come down. He would dine in his house that day. I visited the Upper Room where the Holy Spirit descended on the disciples as they were waiting in the room, praying in one accord. I saw King David's statue with his harp. I equally had the opportunity to visit Lazarus's house and enter the tomb where he was buried then raised from the dead by Jesus Christ.

I went to Canaan, at the place where Christ turned water to wine. There were big pots symbolically on display to commemorate that miracle. In case you visit this site any time, do buy some Canaan wine as a souvenir—they indeed have the best kind of wine. They are duty free, too. I was at the Garden of Gethsemane at Mount of Olives. There, as you look up, you see a very wide and deep valley. Our narrator informed us that some kings and nobles were buried in the valley. It was said that Christ would come back the second time through that valley because it is the same place as explained in Ezekiel Chapter 44 verses 1 to 3, where he talked about the Eastern/Golden Gate. I saw the fig tree that Jesus Christ cursed because at that time He wanted some fruits, but none were found on it. I saw where Jesus taught the disciples how to pray "Our Father, who art in heaven, hallowed be thy name . . ." This prayer was translated in many different languages of the world, evidently displayed as the Lord's prayer written in Yoruba language, a tribe in Nigeria West Africa. I was privileged to participate in the stations of the cross—a journey with Jesus Christ to Golgotha (the place of the skull), from the high priest's place through the market, down to where He was crucified and buried. What a lifetime experience! Astonishingly, we were shown the mark where Jesus Christ stepped before ascending into heaven. These and so many other holy sites were quite soul rejuvenating for me as I felt Jesus Christ's presence as it was, more than 2,000 years ago when he was on earth.

The most thrilling experience—and spiritually fulfilling too—was the morning of the third day in Jerusalem, the day we were expected to depart from Jerusalem to Tiberias to see the Sea of Galilee and other holy sites. I was asked by one of the pastors in our team to lead the morning prayer for the day. Yes, we always had prayer sessions for at least forty-five minutes to one hour every morning before embarking on each day's holy sites visitation. So, the pastor who coordinated the daily devotion (as we had so many pastors in our group, including a bishop), requested I handle the prayer for that day.

I carried out this prayer assignment by humbly requesting God to manifest His power and I recalled most of the holy sites we had visited in Jerusalem. I implored God to grant us the honor of experiencing Christ's presence as it was when He was physically on earth. This was all I prayed, and behold, God instantly honored my prayer request. The power of God descended so mightily, in such a way that no one present could contain. Everyone present in the room experienced the power of God so intently that some people in the chapel were screaming loudly, some falling under the anointing of God. There was a heavy sound of people falling away from their seats. Indeed, everyone got saturated with Christ's presence. I requested God to do so, but to my amazement, I never envisaged that it was going to be so massive.

Later in the day, a pastor among us, who is currently a bishop and general overseer, came to me to inquire if truly I was a Catholic. I told him I am. He asked because he could not fathom how such an irresistible power of God could flow at my request, given that I am a Catholic. He greatly doubted it. He also told me that he overheard some young persons who were among our pilgrim group saying they were so astonished and wondered how the power of God shook everyone present in the chapel while I prayed. I assured him that I did nothing extraordinary. I applied faith in my prayer and only called on God to grant us the privilege of witnessing His power since we were in Jesus's land as written in the Holy Bible, and just as I prayed, God confirmed it. This pastor even appealed that I allow him to establish a church at my location, where I would be a head pastor, because with such power being able to flow through me, being in the Catholic Church might not enable me to explore fully the potential. I declined and assured him that I intend to stay in the Catholic Church to carry out my mission on earth, which is to return drifted souls to God. I assured him that there are so many devoted Catholics who love God sincerely just as I do and who are highly committed in following Christ in truth and in spirit.

Having seen physically and experienced God's power in such a manner, I can attest that indeed the words written in the Bible are true. Glory to God!

Another Amazing Encounter: Restoring the Peace of God in a Couple's Home

During my first visit to the United Kingdom on vacation, I stayed with a couple. This visit happened to be the first time I was meeting this couple. The woman picked me up from the airport and from that moment till we got to her house, she told me her marital life challenges. This discussion continued for hours. She really needed to talk to someone she could be comfortable with, and that person happened to be me, though we were meeting for the first time. I had arrived that day at Heathrow Airport, Terminal 3, having traveled by air for close to seven hours, so I was tired. But watching her so engrossed in pain as she told me so much, I had to listen with keen attention, encouraging her as she expressed her marital plight. Considering all she told me, the most crucial thing was that she had not been on talking terms with her husband for months, though they were living together. He also had not eaten her meals for months. She alerted me not to be bothered should her husband make an unfriendly gesture towards me.

Considering all the worries she expressed, I encouraged her with words and prayed with her from the depth of my heart to suit her troubled state. Just like a soothing balm, by the next day, she ran into the room I stayed in and informed me that her husband inquired why she had not prepared a meal for him. She was amazed that her husband suddenly wanted to eat the food she cooked again. Though she reminded him that he had for months stopped eating her food and was not on talking terms with her, a part of her was so glad that peace had appeared in her matrimonial home. The husband duly apologized to his wife and explained that he did not know why he behaved in that way, as had been the case with them on several occasions. He confessed to her that at certain periods of the month, it appeared certain strange forces would instigate him to pick a quarrel with her.

To the glory of God, my visit to that family became the last of such recurrent and unfortunate incidents. It has been more than ten years and she has never reported such an act from her husband again.

They reconciled and the husband was so friendly when he met me. He made sure he brought me lots of chocolates and other souvenirs as he came back from work throughout my stay with them.

They grew so fond of me, to the point that when my vacation came to an end, her husband showed concern about how it would feel around the house when I left. The wife equally showed her appreciation. She said: "You are the angel God used to restore peace in my home."

Yes, we are the light of the world. Wherever we go, we are required to shine the light. In such a scenario, I invited the Holy Spirit who is God's bearer of light into that home that was in chaos and God manifested His presence. The light showed and expelled the darkness that initially enveloped them.

Pause and Reflect

Throughout history and in our own lives, God reveals Himself in powerful ways—through divine encounters, miracles, and moments that leave no doubt of His presence. These manifestations remind us that He is always near, guiding, protecting, and reassuring us of His unfailing love.

Take a moment to reflect on how God has shown up in your life. Sometimes His presence is evident in grand, supernatural ways, while other times, it's found in quiet moments of peace and provision.

Reflection Questions:

1. Can you recall a moment when you strongly felt God's presence? What impact did it have on your faith?

2. How do you recognize the ways God manifests Himself in your daily life?

3. What biblical stories of divine encounters inspire you the most?

4. In times of doubt or difficulty, how can you remind yourself of God's continued presence?

5. What steps can you take to be more aware and receptive to God's presence in your journey?

Chapter 12

WISDOM PASSED DOWN FROM DAD

"Hear, my son, your father's instruction, and reject not your mother's teaching; A graceful diadem will they be for your head; a pendant for your neck."
Proverbs 1:8–9 (NABRE)

This is a special tribute in memory of my beloved daddy, Sir Eugene Augustine Onyeachufulenwanneya Obiegbu KSJ, who passed away some years ago, but his memories have remained evergreen to me.

Learning from the numerous admonishing stories told to me by my father, he was emphatic about the reason he hardly ate in people's houses or let his guard down. I therefore imbibed that habit and seldom ate indiscriminately.

He never ceased making it clear that he had never taken what did not belong to him. He would say, "I have never picked someone's pin before." Invariably, he inculcated the value of integrity and honesty in his children. This was true of him, not because I could attest to that as his daughter, but it was a known fact by members of every community he had lived in and all places he worked. He said: "A good name is better than riches." Those were his teachings, principles, and endearing ways of parenting. Continue to rest in the bosom of Christ, Paapa, Amen.

As one journeys as a pilgrim, no matter the circumstance you are confronted with, do not forget to uphold your values and show integrity. They are the light you need to see in the dark.

My dad also enshrined in me the admiration for excellence and accuracy. He would always say, "Reading makes a man." He loved to read and acquired knowledge in all subjects. He was called "the Encyclopedia," because he was so versatile that hardly was there any known subject on the face of the earth that he had no in-depth knowledge about. Sometimes I wondered what kind of brain he possessed. This was true to the point that when he passed and then came the day of his burial, an elder in the community who was my dad's maternal relative came to where he laid and talked to him. He requested that my dad should not go to the other side of the divide without relinquishing his brain. My dad's maternal uncle was invariably affirming that my dad had a brilliant brain that was very strange to the entire town.

His zeal to acquire knowledge was a great inspiration to me. All through his lifetime, there was no word I asked my dad about that he had to check in the dictionary. He was the dictionary we all consulted. He would immediately give you the meaning of the word and explain the root of the word or grammatical connotation. When he forgot a word and wanted to recall it, he would recite the alphabet, and once he got to the letter that began the word he was trying to remember, he would immediately remember the word. This has often filled me with astonishment. Presently, when I speak or write, my elder sister calls me "Eugene"—with this, she tries to depict that I am displaying the brilliance of my dad. Equally, my colleagues and professors admire my level of intelligence. However, with every sense of responsibility, I often acknowledge that my level of intelligence is still far below my dad's. Yes, I still say to anyone who admires my expression of wisdom that I am still not at 20% of my dad's brilliance. I am aspiring. Probably, in the future, I will get to that level or surpass it if Christ tarries in coming.

The message here is that, to excel as a gallant pilgrim, you must deliberately and consistently endeavor to acquire good knowledge for your effective application to day-to-day activities of life. Failure to acquire knowledge and apply wisdom leaves one vulnerable to disaster.

He would tell me "Eri eche wu ihe ojoo"—that is, eating while thinking of where the next meal will come from, because one is struggling financially, is a very terrible thing in life. So, he would admonish me that I should always pray against what he called "ike ihi ihii" (according to him, this is a mysterious phenomenon that is more gigantic than an elephant, both in size and strength, and when it comes upon someone, it overpowers the person). It is believed that when such a gigantic circumstance befalls someone, the person will surely be crushed. So, he would advise that one should always pray against such terrible encounters. No one truly deserves to encounter such. However, the twists of life in this world sometimes present things on one's journey that could appear like an "ike ihi ihii" has walked through the person. So, one constantly needs to invoke God's mercy and grace as you take on your Christian journey, and in life generally. This will guide you and grant you the secret tools to excel in life. When you excel, you will not be on the pathway of eri eche.

These teachings and thoughts of my dad contributed to shaping me so immensely. Now he is not in the physical, but whenever I find myself at a crossroads, I draw strength from some of these words relevant for that circumstance in order to realign myself, while calling on God to intervene.

My dad had an eye for details. He would insist while vetting my write-ups that I express my thoughts clearly and I remain accurate both with my grammatical expressions and in spelling. If you missed a letter in someone's name or spelled a name wrongly, for instance, though one could guess what you meant, my dad would insist it cannot be said to be that person. This is because the name has been wrongly spelt even when it is just a letter that is missing. He was indeed meticulous, and I learnt the skill of being meticulous from him. Initially, it was annoying, but when I made peace with doing it right, I noticed the result was always excellent. When your work comes out accurate through appropriate efforts, you sure will always feel good and others will too. Whether they acknowledge this or not.

At the workplace and in all I found myself doing, most of the tenets I picked up from my dad enforced my actions. I knew I had to be aware of what is expected of me, and I must accurately, with speed, deliver excellent results. Nothing short of it. Even when I hide from being noticed, it has always been near impossible not to be noticed and given roles I would ordinarily consider enormous and exalted. Yes, I succeeded because I learnt from the best of the human species—my dad, my Paapa. He inspired me to take on various trainings, some I considered then as disturbances. However, he never gave up. He pushed me to understand the principles of grammar and ensured I wrote correctly. He would correct my write-ups then and instill his principle: "Say what you mean and mean what you say." He said, "I want you to acquire this because the skills would ensure your financial stability. I don't want you to suffer when I am no longer on earth." Then, I didn't quite understand because I was very young, but today, I know better. Thank God my daddy did not give up in ensuring I acquired those skills he considered most important in life. The different levels of university degrees I acquired were products of the skills my dad inspired me to get. These skills have stood the test of time in my attitude toward work, relationships, professions, and life generally.

Some people at various locations and circumstances would ask me, "Are you a teacher?" When I inquire why the question, I sometimes would hear it was because of how I speak, act, or behave.

At this juncture, beloved friends in Christ, I will be narrowing my overflowing thoughts to a close. As for the other thoughts and experiences that were not included in this book, I will equally articulate them and put them in another thrilling book.

Having said this, I want to encourage you that whatever situation may be confronting you on your pilgrim's journey, the information in this book may serve as a boost to your strength and a panacea needed to equip you for the task ahead. Furthermore, if you have not commenced your pilgrim's journey, I implore you to make a bold step today and start this amazing journey in a conscious and deliberate manner.

As you pray along with me, you will experience what is needed to melt whatever challenge may be confronting you. Take a step of faith with total resignation to the will of God and say this prayer:

"Almighty Father and King of All Ages who is the Eternal God, Creator of Heaven and Earth, the One for whom heaven is His throne and the Earth His footstool, the Sanctus Sanctorum, the Trinity in one God, I join the twenty-four elders in heaven to bow in worship and I join the angels to chant holy, holy, holy, is thy name, O Lord God of Host. You know me and what I am going through. I believe that I am made in your image and likeness and deeply desire you in my life. I implore you to grant me the help I need now to overcome the challenges confronting me in my journey of life. I humbly ask that you grant my request as you

behold my broken and contrite heart through Christ our Lord. Amen.

*Child of God, now that you have surrendered your will to God Almighty to direct your affairs henceforth, I make pronouncement on you not only as a divinely converted child of God and fellow pilgrim, but more, as a Jerusalem pilgrim. By the unction of the Holy Spirit, as I lift God's scepter and my divine authority, let there be total transformation in your life. Just as Jesus Christ said to the people at Lazarus tomb, "untie him," and as He said, "little child, rise"—"talitha cumi"—*I say to you, in the name that is above all names, *who is Christ the King, let whatever unfavorable situation before you succumb now to the power of the Master (Rabboni) and may the one praying now with me receive divine freedom and total restoration in the mighty name of Jesus Christ. Amen."*

Chapter 13

MEASURING GROWTH AND PURPOSE

"Teach us to count our days aright, that we may gain wisdom of heart." Psalm 90:12 (NABRE)

As I stood in my house preparing what to eat, I heard the word in my spirit "Ziglar." I never came across any such word prior to this day so I tried to ignore this Ziglar word. It re-occurred through the week, and this got me to dig more into the knowledge behind the word being sent to me by the Holy Spirit.

First, I searched in the scriptures for the word, but what came close to the sound of the word was "Ziklag," a town in Judea. I said to myself that I must stick to what I heard, which was Ziglar. It means bricklayer or brickmaker. In German, it is spelt as Zeigler.

I also discovered that there was a man called Zig Ziglar who was famous for his motivational speeches. I found some of his thoughts very interesting. Some of those that appealed to me were:

- "Getting knocked in life is a given. Getting up and moving forward is a choice."

- "We cannot start over, but we can begin now, and make a new ending."

- "You don't have to be great to start, but you have to start to be great."

- "Life is a zigzag journey, they say, not much straight and easy on the way, but the wrinkles in the map, explorers know, smooth out like magic at the end of where we go."

- "The expert in anything was once a beginner."

- "You have to believe in yourself when no one else does . . ."

These quotes were quite thrilling and got me thinking further about what God was trying to communicate to me by His Spirit.

In putting all my thoughts together, I understood that building a structure is like grooming a life. In structure building, a bricklayer (Ziglar) gathers day by day various bricks and puts them together by laying them one after the other (brick bonding). These various bricks are filled with mortar. At times, the bricklayer removes some bricks that were not properly placed, realigning them with the shape. At the end of this hard work by the bricklayer, despite the mess that comes with the bricklaying or structure building, something magnificent comes out, which is a beautiful, well-colored edifice called a house. This house takes in various people who come in to live in it for shelter. This is awesome.

God was using the nature of a bricklayer (Ziglar) to inform me about the true nature of life. To understand life, it is necessary to understand the work of a bricklayer, then mirror it to your life. I was able to come up with the conclusion that life shapes you, as a Ziglar! Human beings are truly structured in a Ziglar procedure. When you understand this fact, as I was meant to, you can see your failures as part of the structure. When things do not turn your way or when things become difficult, cast your mind to the bricklayer. The Ziglar removes the bricks that need to be removed, realigns the bricks, and sometimes replaces the bricks to get the right shape. The bricklayer remains studious at work, alert, focused, and determined to finish well. The aim of every builder is to see the final product, which is a good house. So, you as a Ziglar must uphold a builder's principle to get to that finished product. A Ziglar does not give up. Everything is put in to have a solid and beautiful structure.

God Almighty is our Ziglar. His Christ is the brick (cornerstone) and the Holy Spirit is the mortar joint. The scripture in Ephesians Chapter 2 verses 20–22 New American Bible (Revised Edition) said: "Built upon the foundation of the apostles and prophets, with Christ Jesus himself as the capstone. Through Him the whole structure is held together and grows into a temple sacred to the Lord, in Him you also are being built together into a dwelling place of God in the Spirit." Also, Matthew Chapter 21 verse 42 (NABRE) states: "Jesus said to them, 'Did you never read in the scriptures: the stone that the builders rejected has become the cornerstone; by the Lord has this been done, and it is wonderful in our eyes?'" Another scripture that buttresses God the Father as the builder (vine grower), Jesus Christ the stone (true vine) and the Holy Spirit a mortar joint (solidifier/witness) is in John Chapter 15 verses 1 to 2 and verse 26 (NABRE). Here it states: "I am the true vine, and my Father is the vine grower. He takes away every branch in me that does not bear fruit, and every one that does he prunes so that it bears more fruit. (V.26) When the Advocate comes, whom I will send you from the Father, the Spirit of truth that proceeds from the Father, he will testify to me."

The work God put into creating human beings and nurturing them from childhood to adulthood both in spiritual journey and physical journey, and the secret behind it, is in this Ziglar assessment. I found that the steps to making bricks were in stages, from mining the clay/sand, which is extracted from the earth just as human beings came from earth, to the stage of grinding and blending the raw materials into fine powder. This is eventually mixed with water to get it ready for use. There is the molding stage; the drying stage; and the firing stage. Then, it reaches the stage of inspection.

Often, I am amazed when I realize how the Holy Spirit reveals mysteries to me using words, signs, sound, air, and just about anything, to educate me in my journey as a pilgrim. The information sometimes is so overwhelming but quite exciting. The beauty behind this is that it opens my eyes to see situations the way they truly are without following the bandwagon aimlessly.

My earnest desire for you is that as you read with an open mind, you will receive the required knowledge that would set you on the path of bliss and in closer relationship with the Holy Spirit of God.

Pause and Reflect

Life is a continuous journey of growth, learning, and self-discovery. Assessing where we are in different areas—faith, relationships, career, and personal development—helps us realign our priorities with God's purpose. Reflection allows us to recognize progress, acknowledge areas for improvement, and seek divine direction for the road ahead.

As you reflect on this chapter, consider how you are measuring your growth. Are you progressing toward the life God has called you to live?

Reflection Questions:

1. What areas of your life reflect the most growth over the past few years?

2. Are there aspects of your life where you feel stagnant or unfulfilled? What steps can you take to change that?

3. How do you balance personal ambition with spiritual purpose?

4. What role does faith play in your decision-making and goal-setting?

5. How can you use self-assessment as a tool to align your life more closely with God's plan?

Chapter 19

THE POWER OF PRAYER

"Therefore, confess your sins to one another and pray for one another, that you may be healed. The fervent prayer of a righteous person is very powerful."
James 5:16 (NABRE)

This chapter has been dedicated fully for prayer. As you use these divinely inspired words to pray, I am convinced that God Almighty will answer as you put your trust in Him. So, pray with faith all or any of these prayers and testify to the glory of God.

Prayer for Forgiveness

This prayer is vital. To prepare your mind and for anyone who may have been hurt, I must state here that it is not easy to forgive, especially when such hurt permeates the heart. For instance, a hurt done to you by a trusted blood relative; a "friend"; someone you have mutual agreement with to uphold trust. It may be likened to the hurt Julius Caesar felt when Brutus plunged the last weapon that killed him. He said: "Et tu,

Brute?" Even you, Brutus? After this kind of hurt, should you survive it and you are told to forgive, it is not an easy path to follow. The worst is when the one who hurt you did not deem it fit to apologize for the hurt or had apologized in the most arrogant manner.

I had several disappointing moments from people at various stages of my life. Most devastating were those involving trusted people—even those from the same Christian fold.

At a certain time, I experienced a betrayal in person which later played out in a dream I had. In this dream, I was with a female friend who told me to come with her down a particular road. I told her that she should allow us to remain close to the beginning of the road so that we would not go so far away from the bus stop. She encouraged me not to worry—it did not matter should we go deeper into the street. So, I trusted her and followed. As we went deeper into the street as I saw in that dream, behold, our bus came. Just as I envisaged, we had drifted far from where we should have stayed and waited for this bus. I saw people scampering into the bus because they stayed close to the stop.

Do you know what this supposed friend did in this dream? On sighting that the bus we were waiting for had come, she ran towards it without considering if I was following or not. Remember, she was the one who misled me from where I was supposed to stand to wait for the bus. When I saw that she was running her own course and totally ignored me, I tried to run and suddenly saw that I could not run as fast as I wanted because I was holding my young son in my hand. That so-called friend abandoned us. I had to walk instead of run because my young son could not run as expected. As we walked, tracing our way back to go and join the bus, behold—everywhere had flooded in such a way that it was difficult to know where the water drainage was, so we had to cautiously trace our way amidst the flood in order not to fall into any danger should we veer off the main road. My son in the dream was agitated on seeing the massive flowing flood we were confronted with. He did not want to walk through the water. However, I encouraged him to brace up. I admonished him that though he was still very young, he might meet more such floods and when they appear, he should never give up but brace up to conquer them as we would conquer this one. Surely, we eventually conquered that flood, whatever it represented at that time of our lives.

As I woke from sleep, I thought over this strange dream and was able to tag it to one or two persons that deceived me, and when the chips were down, they abandoned me. To forgive such persons may be quite difficult because they made me suffer deeply and caused me tremendous loss due to their deceit, whatever reasons could have made them treat me in such a manner.

In this kind of situation, the Spirit of God inspired me to let go of such sad memories. God taught me the word "metanoia" (having a changed mind). I was told that if I hold on to such very sad and disappointing memories, I would invariably be telling God that I did not appreciate all the battles He won for me despite the challenges brought my way. So having in mind that I did not intend to be ungrateful to God, I therefore surrendered all my pains to God and all the sad memories.

You may have been betrayed so badly in different circumstances, or like what I just narrated, and you are feeling that you cannot let go. Remember, I was told, "If you keep up with the sad memories, you are saying to God, 'I do not appreciate your innumerous blessings to me.'" So let go and let God.

Invariably, sincerely forgive those who have hurt you. Ask for pardon from those you have hurt. This is necessary for effective metanoia required for your life journey as a devoted Christian.

1. PRAYER FOR PARDON—2 CHRONICLES 7:14 (NABRE): "If then my people, upon whom my name has been pronounced, humble themselves and pray, and seek my face and turn from their evil ways, I will hear them from heaven and pardon their sins and heal their land."

Oh God my Father and Lord, I acknowledge that I have erred, having searched inwardly. I have done things my way without recourse to you. I have offended those I should be kind to as expected of me. I am ashamed of my actions and sincerely repent of them. Pardon my sins and help me to likewise pardon those against whom I bear grudge. Kindly renew my heart and turn it anew with your refreshing grace that I may live again and be fully restored into your faith and love through Christ our Lord I pray. Amen.

2. PRAYER FOR CONVERSION/RETURN OF SOULS TO GOD— ZECHARIA 1:3 (NABRE): "Say to them, thus says the Lord of Hosts, return to me—oracle of the Lord of Hosts—and I will return to you, says the Lord of Hosts."

Oh God my Father, life without you is meaningless. Life begins with you and ends with you. If I had shown unbelief in any way, I did so out of ignorance. Help me to truly believe. You showed yourself to your disciples and they saw and believed. Do the same for me that I will grow in faith and hope in you the true God. Convert me into whom you have made me to be by the help of your Holy Spirit and keep me for yourself. This I pray through Christ our Lord. Amen.

3. PRAYER FOR RESTORATION—PSALM 71:20–21 (NABRE): "Whatever bitter afflictions you sent me, you would turn and revive me. From the watery depths of the earth once more raises me up. Restore my honour; turn and comfort me."

My Father and Almighty God, the Maker of Heaven and Earth, the Beginning and the End, the One who sits upon Jasper (as

I heard you say in one of the dreams I had), the Restorer of the Dry Bones by your own power, in your infinite mercy and grace, release your love like a rainbow and restore every soul lifted to you now by these words of prayer. No matter how dried these souls or beings are, because they are from you, I implore you to reach them and breathe fresh life back in them. Let them be restored now both spiritually and physically. Let Christ who is King reign in these souls. May the four corners of the earth draw God's breath of creation to renew and restore all these souls back to God in the mighty name of Jesus Christ. Amen.

4. PRAYER OF THANKSGIVING—LUKE 17:11–19 (NABRE): ". .. now one of them, realizing he had been healed, returned, glorifying God in a loud voice, and he fell at the feet of Jesus and thanked Him . . ."

Thank you, my heavenly Father, for making all things well in your time, in your image and likeness. You also saw that all you made was good. Alleluia be to your holy name for all you do for me. I cannot thank you enough. I have been redeemed, called, located, restored, and sustained and my name is written in the book of life—thank you, God Almighty. I deeply want to express my gratitude to you now for those things I somehow assume do not matter. I now know that there is no favor that is little. By these words now, I say I am deeply grateful. For my life, for my family, for my child(ren), for all I have now and still expect, for defending me even while asleep, for your mercy that I received, for always keeping me safe with the help of the angels and saints who watch and pray for me, I bring my offering of unreserved gratitude/thanksgiving. Thank you most immensely for the gift of life and I thank you particularly for this favor I have received and this one I am still expecting, because I have the assurance that you, my God, my heavenly father, reigning forever, are able to do and have done what I have asked. I return all the glory, honor, adoration, and thanksgiving because my thanksgiving has been accepted. Amen.

5. PRAYER FOR DIVINE HEALING—JOHN CHAPTER 5 VERSES 6–9 (NABRE): "When Jesus saw him lying there and knew that he had been ill for a long time, he said to him, do you want to be well? Sir I have no one to put me into the pool when the water is stirred up . . . Jesus said to him, rise, take up your mat, and walk. Immediately the man became well, took up his mat, and walked."

Today, as you look unto Jesus Christ by faith and in total resignation, may Christ who cured the blind, lame, and paralyzed man at the pool of Bethesda heal your infirmities. Now, Christ asks you, do you want to get well? Oh Lord, from your cistern that pours out divine healing water, release your virtue of healing that shows your infinite love and mercy upon this your child who has looked upon you with faith for healing today. May this restoration to good health bring this child of God back to you through Christ our Lord. Amen.

6. PRAYER FOR CHILDREN—MATTHEW 19:14 (NABRE): "But Jesus said, let the children come to me, and do not prevent them; for the kingdom of heaven belongs to such as these."

Our Father in heaven, our Maker and Protector, thank you for the children you gave to us, thank you for their lives from the time of conception to delivery, infancy, teen age, unto adulthood. You indeed know them and have destined them for good purpose. May this good purpose never be truncated by the devices of the evil ones, be they atmospheric, spiritual, or physical. These children, since they are yours, by this prayer are rededicated unto you. Keep them; nurture them; preserve them; bless them exceedingly in all areas of life; let them grow well to know and love you; grant them success and good insight. May they excel to make their parents and nation proud and at the end, after long, fulfilled years on earth, may they return to you in heaven where you live and reign forever. Amen.

7. PRAYER FOR GOD'S ANOINTING—1 SAMUEL CHAPTER 16 VERSE 13 (NABRE): "Then Samuel, with the horn of oil in hand, anointed him in the midst of his brothers, and from that day on, the spirit of the Lord rushed upon David. Then Samuel set out for Ramah."

Oh Lord God Almighty, as you anointed David and your spirit took over him and worked extraordinarily in him as king, warrior, and special minister of God, I pray for a greater outpouring of your oil. Let the power of your presence occupy everyone and put in the heart the light of your salvation which gives life, power, and enthronement as a child of God. Amen.

8. PRAYER FOR CALL TO SERVE—MATTHEW 4 VERSE 19 (NABRE): "And He said to them, come after Me, and I will make you fishers of men."

Life on earth is naturally a call for service. When this is not being done, it indicates a diversion of divine purpose. I pray that as you read this, the burning desire to hear the voice of God will reverberate within you and as you hear Him speak in the best way you can understand, may you receive the grace to obey this call to serve God. Humanity indeed awaits the manifestation of your innate potential.

O Lord, I open my heart to you to receive the grace to follow you. I want to fulfill the purpose of my earthly journey; deliver me when I get distracted with things of this world, do not give up on me when I make a promise to you and find it hard to fulfill. Give me the clarity I need in the face of confusion and the burning zeal to walk along with you, and at the end of my journey here on earth, may I make it into heaven, which is the ultimate goal, through Christ our Lord. Amen.

9. PRAYER FOR THE NATIONS—ZECHARIAH 4:7 (NABRE): "Who are you, O great mountain? Before Zerubbabel you become a plain; He will bring forth the first stone amid shouts of Favor, favor be upon it."

Father, it is your will that all nations shall exist in peace, love, and unity. Whatever threatens these core fundamentals in such a way that the people dwelling in them are confronted with all manner of malady and perils, O God, take such ills away. Kindly protect our nation, keep them safe and filled with your blessings. Amen.

10. PRAYER FOR SPECIAL NEEDS—JOHN CHAPTER 21 VERSE 6 (NABRE): "And He said to them, cast the net on the right-hand side of the boat and you will find something. So, they cast it, and were not able to pull it in because of the number of fish."

May Jesus Christ appear in the situation you most need intervention for as He did unto His disciples, and may you receive instant turnaround for good. Oh, God, do your miracle again in Jesus Christ's mighty name. Amen.

11. PRAYER TO EXPERIENCE GOD'S LOVE—ROMANS 8:38–39 (NABRE): "For I am convinced that neither death, nor life . . . nor any other creature will be able to separate us from the love of God in Christ Jesus our Lord."

Father, you said nothing can separate us from your love and I believe. I pray that you release your love unto this heart beyond human comprehension. May your love bring about total transformation in this heart and every situation in the life of this child of God through Christ our Lord. Amen.

12. PRAYER TO OVERCOME NIGHTMARES—PROVERBS 3:24 (NABRE): "When you lie down, you will not be afraid, when you rest, your sleep will be sweet."

May you lie down and not be afraid. May your sleep be sweet and peaceful. May you be rejuvenated and may the angels of God—the seraphim, the cherubim, the thrones, the dominion, the powers, the virtues, the principalities, the archangels, and the angels—keep constant watch over you. May nightmares be rebuked in your life in the name of Jesus Christ. Sleep and wake in victory through Christ the Lord. Amen.

13. PRAYER FOR EMPLOYMENT—PSALM 127 VERSES 1-2 (NABRE): "Unless the Lord build the house, they labor in vain who build. Unless the Lord guard the city, in vain does the guard keep watch. It is vain for you to rise early and put off your rest at night, to eat bread earned by hard toil—all this God gives to his beloved in sleep."

Oh, dear Lord, because you have said in your Word that I will not toil in vain and you will bless the work of my hand so that I am satisfied, I seek employment that is good in your sight, a job that will enable me to continue to fellowship with you, and as I diligently work, bless the work of my hands through Christ our Lord. Amen.

14. PRAYER TO FINISH THE EARTHLY RACE WELL—2 TIMOTHY 4 VERSE 7 (NABRE): "I have completed well; I have finished the race; I have kept the faith."

May God Almighty supply the fullness of grace to finish this Christian race well, especially amid the battles between the human flesh and the spirit within. May none of the redeemed of the Lord be found unworthy at the time when the roll is eventually called up yonder. Amen.

15. PRAYER FOR GOD'S FAVOR—PSALM 84:11 (NABRE): "For the Lord God is a sun and shield; The Lord gives grace and glory; No good thing does He withhold from those who walk uprightly."

Oh God, I implore you to favor this daughter or son of yours who looks unto you for favor. Your word says you do not deny anything good to those who walk uprightly. The words he/she has heard and believed has made him/her clean. Grant this favor (mention the favor) through Christ our Lord. Amen.

16. PRAYER TO OVERCOME SATANIC ATTACK—LUKE 10 VERSE 19 (NABRE): "Behold, I have given you the power to tread upon serpents and scorpions and upon the full force of the enemy and nothing will harm you."

God our Father, thank you for the power and authority given to us to walk on anything evil, including authority over the power of the enemy. By this, your word is settled, and these enemies are all defeated now. Let them be overpowered and expelled now. Let them lose their hold upon their victims. Let the tied be untied and let there be holistic freedom. May you again break the gates of brass and set the bars of iron put by the enemy asunder in the mighty name of Jesus Christ. Amen.

17. PRAYER FOR FRUITFULNESS—GENESIS 1 VERSE 28: "God blessed them and God said to them: Be fertile and multiply; fill the earth and subdue it. Have dominion over the fish of the sea, the birds of the air, and all the living things that crawl on the earth."

Lord, you said we should increase, multiply, and subdue the earth. Cause increase that brings glory to your name unto this child of God. May there be fruitfulness in all spheres of this child of God. Be fruitful! Amen!

18. PRAYER FOR HAPPINESS—JOHN 7 VERSE 38 (NABRE): "Whoever believes in me, as scripture says: Rivers of living water will flow from within him."

O Lord, grant joy and peace in every troubled mind. Restore happiness and may the Holy Spirit fill your heart with the river of living water who is Christ the King. Amen.

19. PRAYER FOR THE SOULS OF THE DEPARTED—JOHN 11:25 (NABRE): "Jesus said to her, I am the resurrection and the life, the one who believes in Me will live, even if he dies, will live, and everyone who lives and believes in me will never die. Do you believe this?"

Oh God grant your divine mercy above judgement to all the departed family members, friends, colleagues, neighbors, defenders of the country who passed while safeguarding society, and all others in mind at this moment. Eternal rest grant unto them, Oh Lord, and let your perpetual light shine upon them. May they rise in their glorious and shiny robes on resurrection day. May they find peace in the bosom of Christ. Also, grant divine amnesty to the suffering souls in purgatory. Restore the holy innocents to live, I pray through Christ our Lord. Amen.

20. PRAYER FOR CONCEPTION—1 SAMUEL 1 VERSES 9–18 (NABRE): "Hannah rose after one such meal at Shiloh and presented herself before the Lord; at the time Eli the priest was sitting on a chair near the doorpost of the Lord's temple. In her bitterness she prayed to the Lord, weeping freely . . ."

Oh God, for every pain of barrenness, let the power Christ used to destroy evil on the cross by His death and resurrection destroy the yoke of childlessness. Mercy speaks above judgement, therefore, let mercy speak now and restore whatever appears to be the challenge in the body causing the barrenness. Let the virtue of conception envelope this body and let it be as in the case of Hannah when the priest, Eli, spoke unto her. May the power of God be made manifest as it was in the days of Elizabeth the mother of John the Baptist, even unto seemingly impossible cases. I declare over the root of this barrenness the words of the angel Gabriel: "For nothing will be impossible for God" (Luke 1 verse 37 NABRE). So let fruitfulness replace barrenness. Grant this request, O God my Father, and take all the glory. Amen.

21. PRAYER FOR PEACE AND UNITY IN THE FAMILY— EPHESIANS 4:3 (NABRE): "Striving to preserve the unity of the spirit through the bond of peace."

Oh GOD, you instituted the family and cherished communion with it, about which you were clear to say: therefore shall a man leave his father and mother, cleave unto his wife, and they shall become one flesh. But the enemy has fought to destroy this unity from the beginning. Let your mercy speak and restore broken homes, grant peace and unity. Keep the family united in your peace, love, and faithfulness so that your blessings shall continue to abound in this family of God. St. Joseph, the patron saint of families, kindly implores the help of God for unity, peace, and stability in families through Christ our Lord. Amen.

22. PRAYER FOR SCHOOL CHILDREN—PROVERBS CHAPTER 3 VERSE 20 (NABRE): "Walk with the wise and you become wise, but the companion of fools fares badly."

Our heavenly Father, you have shown that children are a blessing from you, and they are to be nurtured and treated with care. Behold the school children and keep them safe always in the palms of your hands. When they are in school, they will always operate with divine wisdom to keep good company and listen to the right teachings. They will differentiate between good and evil and only choose what is good. Grant them the awareness, power, and authority to be out of any harm's way, through Christ our Lord. Amen.

23. PRAYER FOR SAFE PREGNANCY AND DELIVERY—PSALM CHAPTER 22 VERSES 10–11 (NABRE): "For you drew me forth from the womb, made me safe at my mother's breasts. Upon you I was thrust from the womb; since my mother bore me, you are my God."

God Almighty, thank you for this great miracle of conception. You are a God who finishes what you started, and you always finish well. See your daughter through this pregnancy and at the due time of delivery, bring the child(ren) safely from the womb. May the baby/babies and the mother be healthy and alive, through Christ our Lord I pray. Amen.

24. PRAYER FOR DIVINE PROTECTION—PSALM CHAPTER 121 VERSES 7–8 (NABRE) "The Lord will guard you from all evil; He will guard your soul. The Lord will guard your coming and going both now and forever."

May God guard you from all evil and preserve your soul. May He go before you to make a safe way. May He be at your back to shield you. May He be by your right side to uphold you and be at your left side to strengthen you. You shall not falter. You shall walk and not faint on the way, and run but not faint. You shall be entirely protected from all danger as you continually put your trust in God Almighty, in the name of Christ who is Lord and King. Amen.

25. PRAYER FOR FEAR OF GOD—PSALM CHAPTER 33:8 (NABRE): "Let all the earth fear the Lord; Let all who dwell in the world show Him reverence."

May God grant you His grace to fear Him (this means you will be conscious of Him in all you do and walk right by obeying all He expects of you). May this fear of God grant you a humble heart to always know when you are going astray that you may return to God immediately seeking His mercy. As you walk in the fear of God, may the Lord keep you holy, pure, right and acceptable always in His sight through Christ our Lord Amen.

26. PRAYER TO BE ENROBED IN GOD'S GLORY—EZEKIEL 43 VERSES 4–5: "The glory of the Lord entered the temple by way of the gate facing east. Then the spirit lifted me up and brought me to the inner court. And there the glory of the Lord filled the temple."

Almighty God, I implore you to release your glory upon your son and daughter so desirous of you. Manifest your presence exceedingly that this child of God shall be enrobed in your glory, such as when you hovered upon the face of the waters during creation and as seen in the temple by Prophet Ezekiel. This, I ask of you through Christ our Lord. Amen.

Pause and Reflect

Prayer is our direct line of communication with God. It is where we find strength in weakness, clarity in confusion, and peace in the midst of storms. Whether in moments of joy or hardship, prayer aligns our hearts with God's will and reminds us that we are never alone.

As you reflect on this chapter, consider your own prayer life. Are you consistently seeking God, or do you turn to Him only in times of need? How can you deepen your connection with Him through prayer?

Reflection Questions:

1. How has prayer transformed your life or a specific situation you've faced?

2. What challenges or distractions hinder you from maintaining a strong prayer life?

3. How can you develop a habit of consistent and heartfelt prayer?

4. What biblical examples of powerful prayers inspire you the most?

5. How can you encourage and support others in their prayer journey?

CONCLUSION

The journey of faith is not a straight path; it is a winding road filled with valleys of trials, mountains of victories, and rivers of grace that sustain us through it all. As I reflect on the many experiences that have shaped my spiritual walk, I am reminded that our pilgrimage on this earth is not just about reaching a final destination—it is about the transformation that happens along the way. Every testimony, every divine encounter, every moment of struggle and redemption has been part of God's intricate design to mold me into the person He created me to be.

This book has been a deeply personal account of my journey, but I pray that in sharing my story, it has become more than just my own. I hope that my experiences resonate with you, the reader, and that you find within these pages the encouragement to seek God more earnestly, to listen for His voice, and to trust in His perfect plan for your life. If there is one thing that I have learned through the many revelations, dreams, trials, and moments of divine intervention, it is this: God is always present, always speaking, and always guiding those who seek Him with a sincere heart.

Embracing the Call

Looking back, I can see how my life before encountering God was one of ignorance—not just in the worldly sense, but in a deeper, spiritual way. There was a time when I did not fully grasp the reality of God's presence or His calling upon my life. Like many, I was caught in the illusion that I was in control, that my plans were sufficient, and that my way was the best way. But through divine orchestration, I was drawn into His light.

Answering the call to follow Christ was not an easy decision, nor was it a one-time event. It has been a continual process of surrender, obedience, and trust. There were moments when I hesitated, when I questioned, when I resisted. But each time, God's grace met me where I was. He never forced me; He invited me. And in saying yes to Him, my life was forever changed.

Perhaps you, too, have heard His call. Maybe you are standing at the crossroads, wondering if you should step forward in faith or remain where you are, comfortable yet unfulfilled. I urge you—answer the call. Step into the unknown, trusting that God's plans for you are greater than anything you could ever imagine.

Walking Through the Wilderness

Every believer will experience a wilderness season—a time of testing, uncertainty, and refining. The wilderness is not a sign of God's absence; rather, it is often the place where His presence is most profoundly revealed. Just as the Israelites wandered for forty years before reaching the Promised Land, and just as Jesus was led into the wilderness before beginning His ministry, so too must we go through seasons that strip us of self-reliance and deepen our dependence on God.

My wilderness experiences were painful, yet they were also necessary. They taught me endurance, faith, and the importance of waiting on God's perfect timing. There were days when I felt abandoned, when prayers seemed to go unanswered, when the silence was deafening. But in those moments, I learned that faith is not about feeling God—it is about trusting Him, even in the silence. The wilderness is where we learn that God is enough.

If you are in a wilderness season right now, hold on. Do not be discouraged by the dryness or the difficulties. God is refining you, preparing you, strengthening you. He is teaching you to rely on Him alone. And when the season shifts, you will emerge stronger, wiser, and more deeply rooted in His love.

The Power of Divine Encounters

One of the most profound aspects of my journey has been the ways in which God has revealed Himself to me—through dreams, visions, signs in nature, and undeniable moments of divine intervention. Some may dismiss such experiences as coincidences or figments of one's imagination, but I know better. I have seen God's hand too clearly, felt His presence too strongly, and heard His voice too distinctly to ever doubt His reality.

God is always speaking. The question is, are we listening? Are we paying attention to the subtle ways He communicates with us? Sometimes, He speaks through a scripture that suddenly comes alive in our hearts. Other times, it is through a song, a conversation, a dream, or even the stillness of our spirit. Learning to recognize His voice is one of the greatest gifts we can cultivate in our spiritual journey.

If you have ever felt that God is distant, I encourage you to ask Him to reveal Himself to you. Be still. Be open. Be expectant.

He is not a silent God; He is a God who speaks, who leads, who confirms His presence in ways both great and small.

The Role of Grace

None of us deserve the goodness of God, yet He pours out His grace freely. Grace is what has carried me through every season of my life. It has covered my failures, strengthened my weaknesses, and lifted me when I have fallen. It is the unmerited favor of God that transforms ordinary people into vessels of His glory.

One of the greatest misconceptions is that we must earn God's love, that we must be "good enough" for Him to use us. But grace tells a different story. Grace says that even in our brokenness, we are loved. Even in our mistakes, we are pursued. Even in our weakness, we are chosen. The Christian journey is not about perfection—it is about grace. It is about surrendering daily to the One who is perfect so that His strength is made manifest in us.

A Life Transformed

As I bring this book to a close, I am overwhelmed with gratitude for the journey I have traveled. The person I was before encountering God is unrecognizable compared to who I am today. Not because I have achieved anything on my own, but because His presence has reshaped me.

If my story has taught you anything, let it be this: God is real. He is personal. He is deeply invested in your life. He is calling you into a deeper relationship with Him, and He has a purpose for you that is greater than anything you could ever plan for yourself.

No matter where you are in your journey—whether at the beginning, in the midst of trials, or walking in the fullness of faith—know that He is with you. Keep seeking Him. Keep trusting Him. Keep walking forward in faith.

This pilgrimage does not end until we reach our final home in His presence. Until then, let us journey together, strengthened by His grace, guided by His voice, and sustained by His unending love.

May your pilgrim journey be filled with revelation, grace, and the ever-present love of God. Amen.

AUTHOR'S NOTE

"... I want you to follow my Son ..."—and Gerardine E. Obiegbu-Achoronye did.

Now she extends this same invitation to you: *What are you waiting for?* Join her on this exhilarating journey.

You may have read many books, but this one is unique. It is written in the simplest yet finest language—words that seem to flow from a divine source, imbued with the wisdom of heaven. Coming across this book is truly a once-in-a-lifetime privilege. It is organic, divinely inspired, and filled with revelational knowledge meant for spiritual nourishment and holistic education.

The content is enriching and serves to rekindle the very essence of human existence. It is a practical tool, a spiritual compass, designed to guide readers toward fulfilling the true purpose of life.

Within its pages are specially inspired messages that illuminate the importance of the wilderness experience in one's spiritual development, the unfailing nature of God's faithfulness, and a deeper revelation of the parable of the sower. The author also shares powerful testimonies of what God has done in the lives of others through her obedience.

The book highlights unique signs and symbols through which God has communicated with her—birds, double rainbows, markings in the sky, and more. These divine signs serve as anchors of faith throughout her journey.

Additionally, various heartfelt prayers have been included to offer readers spiritual reinforcement. Without a doubt, God will use these prayers to perform unprecedented miracles in the lives of those who approach them with sincere faith.

As the saying goes, *"The taste of the pudding is in the eating."* Read this book and you will be amazed by the wealth of knowledge, wisdom, and profound spiritual encounters generously revealed for the benefit of humanity.

ABOUT THE AUTHOR

Gerardine E. Obiegbu-Achoronye (JP) holds a bachelor of science in government and public administration, as well as a master's degree in public administration with a specialization in personnel management. She is a highly experienced Human Resources professional with a distinguished career spanning more than two decades. Regarding her career, she served as an Administrative Officer to various management executives across several departments, including Training and Administration, Environmental Services, Engineering and Safety Services, Finance and Accounts, and Human Resources. She grew through the ladder of her career and headed various sections in the Federal Airports Authority of Nigeria, where she rose to the position of Assistant General Manager, Training and Human Resources Development/Training Administrator. In all these roles, she demonstrated excellence and dedication to her duties.

Currently, Gerardine works in the Production Department of the leading meal kit company in the United States.

She has undergone numerous management training programs, one of which was with the globally recognized International Air Transport Association (IATA), where she graduated with distinction. Gerardine is a certified management trainer and holds fellowship memberships in several prestigious professional institutes. She is also an active member of various management and training organizations.

Committed to lifelong learning, Gerardine continues to pursue certifications in areas such as security, healthcare, and safe food handling. She is a certified life coach and a proud member of the International Coaching Federation (ICF). In addition to her professional pursuits, she volunteers in the human services sector.

A devoted and baptized Catholic, Gerardine is a charismatic preacher of God's Word, a passionate prayer warrior, a wife, and a mother.

The Pilgrim's Journey is a culmination of over twenty years of her thoughts, divine revelations, personal experiences, and inspired teachings. This book offers an in-depth reflection of her journey as a Christian pilgrim—detailing the challenges she encountered, the ways in which God refined her, and how He ultimately salvaged her life for His divine purpose.

Readers who absorb the book's captivating stories will be left with hearts melted by God's love and filled with gratitude—not only toward Him but also toward this remarkable, prolific writer. Gerardine is truly a rare gem, a vessel chosen by heaven for the Master's service.

The inspiration to share her knowledge and experiences through writing came to her many years ago. For ten years, she diligently worked on this book. In 2023, she received a divine mandate from the Holy Spirit to complete and publish *The Pilgrim's Journey*. And now, to the glory of God the Father Almighty, the book is finally here.

ACKNOWLEDGEMENT

"But now, thus says the Lord, who created you, Jacob (Gerardine) and formed you Israel; Do not fear, for I have redeemed you; I have called you by name: you are mine. When you pass through waters, I will be with you; through rivers, you shall not be swept away. When you walk through fire, you shall not be burned, nor will flames consume you." Isaiah 43:1–2 (NABRE)

The Pilgrim's Journey is a deeply spiritual and reflective Christian memoir chronicling my personal transformation from a life of ignorance to one of profound faith. Through vivid personal testimonies, biblical references, dream interpretations, and divine encounters, I have shared my evolving relationship with God. It has been highly inspired by the Holy Spirit, to whom I owe all my intellectual and charismatic abilities.

Furthermore, readers of this book will acquire knowledge on spiritual awakening from ignorance to enlightenment; the power of divine calling and obedience; revelations through dreams, symbols, and natural phenomena; the presence and intervention of God in everyday life; the significance of grace, humility, and perseverance in faith; intercession of the Blessed Virgin Mary; God as both a personal guide and a provider; etcetera.

I couldn't have reached this milestone without the help of people and institutions, too numerous to mention. Notwithstanding, I'm compelled to mention a few while not in any way undermining the paramount roles played by others that were not mentioned.

First, my unflinching gratitude goes to God Almighty, the One who dwells in Jasper and causes dry bones to come back to life. I bow in awe and say thank you immensely for using me, unworthy as I am to be an instrument for your kingdom work, and for pushing me to write and publish this life-changing book.

For my lovely family, immediate and extended, I owe unalloyed gratitude. I could not have made it this far without them. Your love strengthens me, and the strong Christian principles embedded in me from childhood through my adulthood have shaped me in no small way as a pilgrim on this divine path. Special mention goes to my son, Emmanuel Achoronye, who has weathered some storms with me even as a child with great tenacity and enduring countenance of optimism in all things. His invaluable personality kept me going at those times I felt quite low, and in such moments, I would hear him utter some words: "Mommy, God bless you"; "Mommy, are you okay?"; "I'm sorry, Mommy, it's okay"; "Take it easy, Mommy"; and so on. He is indeed an awesome child, a forerunner who has helped to illuminate my pathways. He is a divine gift from God that brought significant breakthroughs in my life.

To my Christian fellowship brethren, the Catholic Charismatic Renewal of Nigeria both national and in diaspora, I say a very big thank you for my spiritual development with anointed biblical teachings and prayers spanning over twenty-five years, yet still going. On this, I make special mention of my highly charismatic mentors whose zeal for the work of God has contributed in no small way to bring about true repentance, total divine healing, deliverance, and deeper love for God. These mentors have been used by God directly and indirectly to resuscitate my dripping spirit, especially when I am most in need, through their countless, relentless, powerful preaching and prayers. They are: Rev. Fr. (Dr.) Camillus Ejike Mbaka; Rev. Fr. (Dr.) Anthony Mario-Ozele (Fr., the Friends-In-Christ monthly program years back, was really a life changer for me; through that program, I became one of the few saved from the Lagos Ikeja Cantonment Bomb blast that saw to the gruesome death of thousands of Lagos inhabitants and several wounded); Rev. Fr. Mario Dibie; Rev. Fr. Emmanuel Chibuzor Obimma (Ebube Muonso).

To my ever-smiling dear friend and Christian sister, Dr. Perpetua Emeagi, this acknowledgement will not be complete without expressing how grateful I am for taking time out of your busy schedule to judiciously review this book and for giving that thought-provoking endorsement. May God reward you and thank you.

Special mention will also go to Ms. KeriLynn Lowenstein, who agreed to write the foreword of the book with short notice despite her several engagements. Thank you so immensely and may God count this rewardable service sufficient enough to grant her eternal blessings.

To my parish priest of the Sacred Heart of Jesus Catholic Church and the entire worshipping community, thank you for your warmness and good sense of community fellowship. I must equally mention that the time granted me by the priest to discuss my book when it was at the manuscript stage was appreciated and invaluable.

Also, to all my professional colleagues past and present, who are considered extended family members, I say thank you so much for your warmness, acceptance, love, understanding, training, and retraining during the course of discharging my duties. These have made me feel special and deeply inspired in readiness to give back to the society—on a bigger platform—my undisputable wealth of experience and excellent knowledge acquired over these years.

To all my New Jersey friends, well-wishers, and neighbors, I express my profound appreciation to you. You at various occasions in my life have played big roles to ensure that I felt at home, cherished, loved, and protected. You have been my beacon in the night and from the first day my feet walked on this land, I felt the embrace of a loving mother that said to me, welcome home. I have great love for you, O Garden State, the place of my peace.

Finally, to Reea Rodney, the founder of Dara Publishing, self-publishing expert, and book coach, and her team, who went above and beyond to give this book great professional structure, and moreso for the invaluable friendship that blossomed from the first day we met, which only goes to prove that our paths were divinely orchestrated. This meeting eventually has given birth to this strong, unique, soul-lifting spiritual book. God bless you all so exceedingly.

Gerardine E.Obiegbu-Achoronye

Thank You for Reading

Thank you for taking the time to journey with me through these pages. I pray that The Pilgrim's Journey has inspired, encouraged, and drawn you closer to God.

If this book has blessed you in any way, I would be truly grateful if you left a positive review on Amazon. Your feedback helps others discover the message and makes a big difference in spreading the word.

With heartfelt gratitude,

Gerardine.